PRAYING WITH THE HEART

The Little Way to Jesus

Jean Khoury

PRAYING
WITH THE HEART

The Little Way to Jesus

✝

✵ Angelico Press

Cover image: Simon Bening (Flemish, about 1483–1561)
The Worship of the Five Wounds
Folio from the Prayer Book of Cardinal Albrecht
of Brandenburg, ca. 1525–1530
Cover design: Michael Schrauzer

CONTENTS

Introduction

The Aim of This Book

This book presents the Prayer of the Heart and represents a direct call from Our Lady to develop our intimacy with Jesus Christ and to discover his constant love for us. Without this experience, life loses its meaning and savor. The Prayer of the Heart opens us up to new horizons. This book explains in a practical way how to begin the Prayer of the Heart and helps us in its practice.

The characteristic of this book is that it shows for the first time and in a clear, plain and practical way the inner movement of this prayer. Its goal is to help the reader—as much as a written text can do—to learn what to do practically in order to achieve a real connection with God in one's heart. It provides explanations about this connection and shows the conditions for its mechanism to be successful.

Often spiritual writers give general explanations about the Prayer of the Heart, though they rarely go into its practical details. While we have a great need to know what we have to do in order to receive God and in order to become immersed in him, we also need to know how to let him transform us with the luminous beam of his love. An interest in the explanation of this inner movement is not a superficial matter; rather, its pursuit is vital to the life of any human being.

✛

This book doesn't offer a new way of practicing the Prayer of the Heart. The only aim of the book is to explain this traditional type of prayer in a more understandable way, using diagrams as well as examples. This contemporary explanation is not in contradiction with the ancient ones, but it will help the modern reader to better understand the practice of the Prayer of the Heart. There are amazingly rich treasures in the teachings of the ancient spiritual masters, but the cultural distance between those masters and us makes it difficult for us to understand, appreciate, and benefit from them. This book seeks to fill this cultural gap.

This publication is for everyone, especially for the faithful. There are two reasons for this: 1) The Prayer of the Heart is of vital necessity—as we will see later. 2) All the faithful are introduced into the life of the Trinity through Baptism, which is the exact purpose of the Prayer of the Heart. The book is useful as well to all those who deal with spiritual formation, who can draw on the simplicity and precision of its teaching.

Since we are created "in the image and likeness of God," we find in the depths of our being a thirst to "drink" God and to be nourished by him. God, in turn, is thirsty for us and would like to give himself in earnest to us. He is the one who takes the initiative to love us: he calls us repeatedly, with a gentle voice. Christ came to give us divine life, that is, the Holy Spirit, and we always need to be aware of what we need to do in order to receive Him daily. This is why we pray: "Give us this day our daily bread." In this book we will learn how to "eat God" and how to let him eat us (God is a "consuming fire").

I prefer to use the expression Prayer of the Heart and not "the Jesus Prayer," "meditation," or "mental prayer," because this prayer is at the same time and inseparably: 1) the core of each prayer we make and is necessary to the inner disposition of heart we require in order to make our prayers effective ("lift up your hearts"); and 2) a type of prayer which we carry out at a specific time during the day. We will return to this.

Definition, Necessity, and Benefits of the Prayer of the Heart

We may define the Prayer of the Heart as an inner act in which we offer ourselves to God, who then comes, takes us, and immerses us in his Being, pouring into us the fire of his love. In each Mass, the priest reminds us of that act: "lift up your hearts," and by "up" he means to Christ who is seated at the right hand of the Father. As we see, the Prayer of the Heart introduces us into the Son, who is before the Father, with the Holy Spirit. This type of prayer is intimately related to the altar of the Body and Blood of Christ as well as to Communion itself.

✝

We should practice the Prayer of the Heart at, at least, two different moments:

A) As an inner act that permeates all types of prayer, the Prayer of the Heart should be practiced all the time because we are invited by God to pray all the time in order not to be separated from Christ: "Pray without ceasing" (1 Thessalonians 5:17) and "dwell in Me" (John 15:4).

B) The Prayer of the Heart is also a specific type of prayer, to which we should dedicate some time on a daily basis, in the morning and in the afternoon/evening: 15, 30, or even 60 minutes. The Western spiritual tradition invites consecrated persons to practice the Prayer of the Heart for 30 minutes in the morning and 30 minutes in the evening as a minimum.

✝

The first characteristic of the Prayer of the Heart is that just as at the heart of all types of prayer—such as the Mass, Divine Office, the recitation of the rosary, Eucharistic Adoration—, an inner movement is necessary in order to make the prayer effective, so, too, must this occur with the Prayer of the Heart. This inner act allows any prayer to enter into direct contact with God in the depths of our heart. During this communication, God nourishes us with himself, allowing an effective exchange to take place: we offer ourselves to him, and he offers himself to us.

Seeing the Prayer of the Heart in this way, initially as an inner movement, characterizes and permeates all types of prayer. For this reason we can begin to understand why it is necessary to master this movement in order to be able to enter into the mystery of any real and effective prayer. All prayer should be offered "in Spirit and Truth" (John 4:23), which means in the Holy Spirit and in Jesus who is the Truth: "the hour is coming, and now is, when the true worshipers will worship the Father in spirit and truth, for such the Father seeks to worship Him. God is Spirit, and those who worship Him must worship in spirit and truth" (John 4:23–24).

The second characteristic of the Prayer of the Heart is that it is a type of daily prayer amongst others. That is, the Prayer of the Heart is a specific, distinct prayer, which can stand alone, in the same way as the Mass, the Divine Office, and the rosary do. This type of prayer can be short (an "arrow" prayer) or long (for example, 15, 30, 60 minutes, twice a day or more).

The short practice of the Prayer of the Heart (an arrow prayer) should impregnate our whole day, keeping us more united to Jesus Christ and allowing Him to transform our lives. During the day we should repeat the inner act as much as we can, immersing ourselves in God, letting ourselves be nourished by his Being. The long practice of the Prayer of the Heart, on the other hand, is an encounter with Jesus in which we do not do any other thing except the inner act. In the long practice, we dedicate two occasions (or more) each day, morning and evening, for this encounter, thereby giving Christ supremacy in an absolute manner, not only in our life in general, but during the day as well. The long practice/exercise is a real spiritual meal.

✝

The Prayer of the Heart, however, cannot be separated from another form of prayer, *lectio divina*. Both types of prayer are our two legs which allow us to walk and grow in Christ. As *lectio divina* is the continuation of the Table of the Word in the Mass, the Prayer of the Heart is the continuation of the Table of the Body and Blood of Christ. We cannot separate the one from the other.

The Prayer of the Heart is not a new type of prayer. As we have said, the Prayer of the Heart allows us to really live in the Trinity—in the Son, before the Father, through the Holy Spirit. It enacts the grace of Baptism which is intended to allow us to immerse ourselves totally in the Father, in the Son, and in the Holy Spirit. It allows us to truly worship "in Truth and Spirit" (John 4:23), that is, in Christ who is the Truth and in the Holy Spirit. We see in this way that the Prayer of the Heart is not a new type of prayer but is the core of prayer. Without it, even if we are "praying" we are alienated from the Trinity; therefore our prayer loses its Christian nature and effectiveness. It is the duty of each Christian to enact the grace of his/her baptism by practicing the Prayer of the Heart; otherwise baptismal grace will remain a buried seed, passive, with no life in it. Without the Prayer of the Heart, baptism and Christian life can become a source of pride, bearing no fruit. This sterility is dangerous because God gave us this life on earth in order to bear fruit, fruit that will remain for all eternity.

It is important to practice the Prayer of the Heart because it allows us to activate, with the grace of God, the Seed of Baptism, which is our life in Christ. Thus Jesus invites us continuously to "dwell in him" (see John 15:4) and he warns us very pointedly against doing anything apart from Him: "apart from me you can do nothing" (John 15:5). This means that we have to use our freedom in the right way, that is, by always practicing the Prayer of the Heart so that we can dwell in Him and so that all our acts and work can proceed from Him. This is why it is not merely important to practice the Prayer of the Heart; indeed, there is a radical necessity to practice it, and he who says the opposite has a poor understanding of spiritual life and of the ways to holiness.

We should be very wary of following any spiritual director who fails to mention the Prayer of the Heart, as St. Teresa of Avila warns us in many places in her *Autobiography*. As St. John of the Cross says, "whoever flees the Prayer of the Heart flees all that is good." And, "Do not omit the Prayer of the Heart for any occupation, for it is the sustenance of your soul." He also encourages us to "Never give up the Prayer of the Heart, and should you find dryness and difficulty, persevere in it for this very reason. God often desires to see what love your soul has and love is not tried by ease and satisfaction."

The Prayer of the Heart is for everybody. Indeed, everyone who has been baptized has a heart, a will, and a freedom, and God gives everyone the general help of his Grace so that they can use their freedom and offer themselves to him. We can deduce from this that the Prayer of the Heart is for everybody. The same applies to receiving Communion.

God created the heart of the human to be free (even the heart of the sinner), and at anytime, in any situation, one can cry out to God. In baptism the human being is given the capacity to participate in Christ's Priesthood; therefore, one has within reach on any day or at moment a Priestly capacity, a capacity that allows one to offer oneself in Christ, an acceptable offering to God, in the fire of the Holy Spirit. For all these reasons the Prayer of the Heart is for everybody.

As a type of prayer, the Prayer of the Heart is present in both the Eastern and Western Christian traditions of prayer. In Eastern traditions the Prayer of the Heart might have a number of forms: the Jesus Prayer, ejaculatory prayer, or the short prayers (arrow prayer) of the desert monks. The Western traditions call it mental prayer, sometimes meditation. Some types of prayers that are similar to it are the Adoration of the Blessed Sacrament, praying the Rosary with no mysteries, spiritual communion, and ejaculatory prayer.

The Prayer of the Heart is intimately and vitally linked to the core of our Christian life, therefore their sources coincide. The Prayer of the Heart produces:

1) The activation of the grace of **Baptism**, which is about being immersed in Christ.

2) The activation of the **Priesthood of the Faithful**, which proceeds from our baptism: our capacity to offer ourselves to God.

3) The activation in us of the sacrament of **Confirmation** and helping it to bear fruit. "He breathed on them" (John 20:22).

4) The extension of the grace of **Communion**, impregnating the entire day. "He who eats my flesh and drinks my blood dwells in me, and I in him" (John 6:56).

5) The means to help us to **dwell** in Christ. It is the very application of the act: "dwell in me" (John 15:4).

6) To pray **unceasingly**, as Christ asked us to do in St. Luke's Gospel (Luke 18:1), and as St. Paul invites us: "pray unceasingly" (1 Thessalonians 5:17).

Somebody who is already serving in his/her parish and prays regularly might be thinking: why should I have to add a new exercise, that is, adding the Prayer of the Heart to my daily prayer regime? There are two answers to this question.

First, we cannot describe the Prayer of the Heart as a "new exercise" because it is above all the core of all prayers, and without it there is no prayer. Before setting up a specific time to practice the Prayer of the Heart exclusively, we need to understand that it embodies an inner movement which impregnates all types of prayer since it allows us to really enter into Christ, who is before the Father, in the Holy Spirit. For this reason, nourishing our prayer by it is not the addition of a new exercise, but the infusion of a new vitality and fruitfulness in our prayer. With this inner act, God outpours himself in us and this completely changes the characteristics of any prayer. Therefore, this inner addition is necessary and not optional.

Second, the Prayer of the Heart is considered to be a separate exercise as well; that is, a specific type of prayer to which we daily dedicate time. In order to understand and accept this exercise and not to consider it as "new" or "added," we need to understand its source. The Prayer of the Heart is the extension of the act of Communion, and it helps activate its effects in our life. In fact, the time we dedicate to Communion and immediately after it during Mass is very short, just a few minutes. The work that God is trying to effect in us during the minutes that follow is constricted by the time and space we offer him. It is possible for any human being to increase this space and this time, by remaining in silence, either immediately after Mass or at any other time during the day. This is what we call the Prayer of the Heart. The Prayer of the Heart is a personal decision to give "space" (time and space) to the last Communion we had so that it can act in us with greater and lasting fullness. In this sense, we cannot separate the Prayer of the Heart—understood as a time consecrated to God—from the very moment of Communion during the Mass. Nobody can negate the value and the necessity of Communion, since Christ himself set up the intimate relationship between Communion and the fact of *dwelling in him.* Communion has an absolute influence on our capacity to dwell in Christ, for "He who eats my flesh and drinks my blood abides in me, and I in him" (John 6:56).

Dwelling in Christ is a vital necessity which has eternal consequences: "He who abides in me, and I in him, he it is that bears much fruit, for apart from me you can do nothing" (John 15:5). The Prayer of the Heart, by going back to the very moment of our last Communion—back to the reserve of Christ's Body treasured in our depths—is a unique act of "dwelling in Christ." The human being is like the branches and has the capacity to choose (by practicing the Prayer of the Heart) to attach himself to the Vine (John 15:5). After Communion, if we do not persevere in dwelling in Jesus using the Prayer of the Heart, then the branches will separate from the vine and the sap will not reach them. Communion sustains and causes the human being to grow "like a tree planted by streams of water, that yields its fruit in its season, and its leaf does not wither. In all that he does, he prospers" (Psalm 1:3). The act of Communion connects the roots with the water, while forgetting Communion during the day is equivalent to cutting the connection between the roots and the water. He who turns prayer into a mental exercise using mere words and thoughts, forgetful of involving at the same time the inner movement of the heart, cuts the trunk from the roots.

People who already pray the Divine Office, the rosary, any other prayer, or who adore the Blessed Sacrament, might ask themselves if all these prayers are the same as practicing the Prayer of the Heart. If we consider the inner aspect of the Prayer of the Heart—the act in which we elevate our heart to God and he receives it and places it in his—the answer to this question is that we need to raise up our heart to him so it becomes the core of any prayer.

Since they are forms of pure worship, some types of prayer are characterized by total silence, for instance in the Adoration of the Blessed Sacrament. In this case, adoring the Blessed Sacrament or practicing the Prayer of the Heart is roughly the same. Therefore each person needs to learn the art of the Prayer of the Heart in order to become capable of lasting a long time through distractions that often occur during this silence. It is obvious that he who did not learn to practice the Prayer of the Heart and how to resist the temptations of the mind, of the imagination and of the exterior senses, will sadly tend to transform the hour of Adoration into vocal prayers said together, or into hymns, or even worse: into mental meditation or personal reading. Unfortunately, during Adoration we often pray out loud and sing hymns; rarely are we attentive to the extreme richness of these moments and Jesus desire to immerse each one of us in the fire of his love. Undoubtedly, silent prayer needs to be taught! Leaving it to pure spontaneity amounts to negligent and careless behavior; therefore, we need to correct our understanding of what we practice in order to allow it to bring forth its rich fruits.

If we consider the Prayer of the Heart as a separate exercise and we do not exchange it for any other exercise (such as Adoration), we will not be able to live without it. We need to make time in order to practice it during the day.

✝

Now, let us compare going to Mass daily and the practice of the Prayer of the Heart. He who goes to Mass every day really does a great thing! Indeed, "the Eucharist is the source and summit of the Christian life" (*Catechism* 1324). The highest point in the second part of the Mass is the very moment of Communion. This very moment is short in time, and in itself gives little scope for Jesus to work in us, transforming us into Him. Therefore, we need to extend it through both short exercises of the Prayer of the Heart during the day and a dedicated longer period of time for it. Communion is not a "magic" act; its effect on the rest of the day does not come spontaneously and automatically. The fact that Jesus enters within our being with his Body and Blood does not mean that he acts—and will act—without our collaboration. If the grace of Communion is given to us, receiving it and dwelling in it depends on us—of course, with the help of the grace of God. The one does not contradict the other, but they in fact complement one another. If the reception of Communion in us generates a very powerful thrust in us, dwelling in this thrust depends on us. And to support this teaching and give it efficiency, we need to remember Jesus's words: "He who eats my flesh and drinks my blood dwells in me, and I in him" (John 6:56) linked to Jesus asking us at various times to "dwell in me" (John 15:4) thus insisting on the necessity to remain in this grace.

In conclusion, we can say that if on the one hand the nourishment included in the Mass is complete, on the other hand it depends on us to digest it, assimilate it and work upon it and with it. This comes through practicing the Prayer of the Heart.

✝

The Prayer of the Heart has an efficient and positive influence on our body, our soul and our spirit. Each part of our being benefits in its own way from the grace of God communicated during the Prayer of the heart. This influence is vital. Let us look at them, one by one, from the least important in the eyes of God (the body) to the most important (the spirit).

The Body

The Prayer of the Heart offers several benefits to the body:

1) It eliminates fatigue and stress, resulting from our daily life. It also induces a state of physical relaxation in us.

2) It triggers deep physiological changes: decreases metabolism, blood pressure, heartbeat, rate of breathing, and slows brain waves.

3) It has a positive influence on certain ailments: high blood pressure, diabetes, migraine, back pain, and so forth.

The Soul

The Prayer of the Heart also provides benefits to the soul. Indeed, our lives become meaningless without this relationship:

1) It has a considerable calming effect on the soul. God pours out his peace, a peace which has no equivalent on earth. This peace increases proportionally with our purification.

2) The Prayer of the Heart helps remove the clutter in the mind, bringing to it clarity and order. In addition, it helps to strengthen our will and discipline our imagination.

3) Through it Jesus heals the numerous wounds of our emotions and fills us with a unique and inimitable love.

4) Among other things, it helps reduce anxiety, excess of anger and aggressiveness, mild and moderate depression, and exhaustion.

5) Through it God purifies us and frees us from many different types of slavery, sins and attachments, since during the Prayer of the Heart he works in the very depths of our being where no one can reach by his own efforts.

6) In it, God clarifies the events of the day and makes them appear clearly in front of us, allowing us to see them with his eyes.

7) Through it God completes in us the virtues that start to take form in us through *lectio divina*.

8) In it, God reconciles us interiorly with our enemies and dissolves with his grace all the impurities in our relationships.

9) With the Prayer of the Heart we practice our first ministry and service. It allows us to receive our neighbor into our heart and give him to God through prayer, forgiveness, and by blessing him.

The Spirit

Finally, the Prayer of the Heart provides us with spiritual benefits:

1) It allows a direct connection between our spirit and God. This is the core of any type of prayer. Without this direct connection prayer is not possible. It introduces us into God and through it he gives himself to us.

2) With it, God nourishes us of himself, transforming us in him and making us grow in him. The new man—or Jesus in us—grows in us.

3) The Holy Spirit forms in us the "likeness" of God which we lost through Original Sin.

PART I: The Principal Elements of the Prayer of the Heart

In this first part of the book we will address the different elements or principles of the Prayer of the Heart. This part could seem abrupt, since we won't see the elements working until we reach the second part. Even so, it is an important part because it lays the foundations of a good working Prayer of the Heart. One needs to have a minimum of knowledge and understanding of each element in order to see its correct place in the "puzzle."

The principles of the Prayer of the Heart are: 1) our heart; 2) Jesus; 3) the action of the Holy Spirit; 4) our role; 5) the role of Our Lady; 6); the role of the spiritual master and of the spiritual director. It is important to know the different principles of the Prayer of the Heart and their contents in order for us to deal with them with greater awareness and responsibility. These principles should come together and work together in synergy. If one of them is lacking, it might have a negative influence on the efficiency of the Prayer of the Heart and on the sustainability of its practice.

Our Heart

Let us consider now where the Prayer of the Heart happens. As we said, the Prayer of the Heart makes a direct connection possible between the human being and God. This connection is of the same nature as the connection which occurs between the human being and Jesus who is God at the moment of Communion and is a prolongation of it. We need to be aware that we do not feel this connection with the uncreated nature of Jesus directly and this is proof that it happens in the depths of our being (our heart) and that it occurs in an area which is beyond (higher than) consciousness/perception. In fact, the human being is like a high mountain that has two parts:

1) The upper one, the heart or spirit, pierces the clouds and sees the sun (God) directly and receives its beneficial rays. This part is supra-conscious.

2) The lower one, the soul/body, does not see or sense the sun directly; it does not see directly what is happening between the heart of the human being and God. This part consists of the awareness of the soul and body.

The Prayer of the Heart happens in the heart of the human being when he drinks the Divine Water from God directly, the Holy Spirit (see John 4:10).

Jesus's Place in the Prayer of the Heart

It is possible to consider that the human being is composed of two parts, the exterior one, which is rough (the body), and an interior part, which is more refined and elevated (the spirit). Often the human being lives with his body and senses, attentive to what is happening around him and hardly paying any attention to the presence of an immense inner world inside him. He barely exercises himself in that world, which makes it difficult for him to enter. The condition of prayer is to go into the inner room, to enter this inner world that has Jesus as its center: "when you pray, go into your room and shut the door and pray to your Father who is in secret" (Matthew 6:6). On the cross Jesus opened the door for us between the two worlds, the exterior one and the interior one, and with his blood he broke into our hardened heart and opened a "new way" (see Hebrews 10:20; John 14:6) that leads to him and to Life with him. This is why Jesus said: "I am the door" (John 10:7), "I am the way" (John 14:6), and "I am the Life" (John 14:6). By saying "I am the Life" Jesus means that he is our life, alluding to our union with him and the outpouring of his Holy Spirit in us; this happens during the Prayer of the Heart.

Jesus's place in the Prayer of the Heart occupies exactly the same place as he has in our Christian life. Since he is at the same time perfect God and perfect man, he constitutes everything for us; he is our All, since all the treasures of wisdom and knowledge are hidden in him (see Colossians 2:3) and "in him the whole fullness of deity dwells bodily" (Colossians 2:9).

Furthermore, Jesus gives us the Holy Spirit from the Father; therefore, becoming close to him and being united to him fills us with the Holy Spirit who is the source of our sanctification and transformation in him. For this reason, St. Paul invites us to dwell constantly in Christ who is at the right hand of the Father (see Colossians 3:3), because he is our Temple (see Hebrews 10) wherein we should dwell. St Paul emphasized this concept on numerous occasions, often using the expression "in Christ." Since the first generation, Christians are used to "lift up [their] hearts" to remain in Jesus seated at the right hand of the Father. We find the trace of this early general recommendation in the Mass. We thereby perceive that both the meaning and goal of receiving the body of blood of Jesus in Communion is to allow us to dwell in Jesus (see John 6:56).

The goal of the Prayer of the Heart is to allow us to dwell in Jesus, so that we can receive the waters of the Holy Spirit and worship God the Father "in Spirit and Truth" (John 4:23-24), in the Holy Spirit and in Jesus who is the Truth (see John 14:6).

The Action of the Holy Spirit in the Prayer of the Heart

The Holy Spirit works in the human being, offering two types of help: 1) general help; 2) particular help.

> *General help* is a grace offered to all human beings (even sinners) so that they can enact their will and freedom, thereby expressing their personal decisions and choices. With this general grace, given to everybody, the human being can decide to ask God for his particular help, in a fervent prayer.

> *Particular help* is the Holy Spirit, Comforter, Giver of Life himself, who can sanctify the human being and change him. This is the grace given, the grace which Jesus came to give us. We can call it "the Gift of God" (John 4:10).

Using general help allows us to ask God for particular help. General help, through the grace of God, is given to all of us. Making use of it is always within our reach: it is our duty to use it and it will not happen without our participation. God does not give us particular help (the Holy Spirit himself) if we do not ask for it. This is why Jesus stressed the necessity for us to use the general help of the grace of God with great insistence, saying, "Ask, and it will be given you; seek, and you will find; knock, and it will be opened to you" (Matthew 7:7). When we ask, seek, and knock we activate the general help of the grace of God in us (whether we are aware of it or not). Jesus explained that it is the Holy Spirit that we should ask for (see Luke 11:13 and John 14:13-17).

For example, if we want to forgive a person who has offended us, we find it impossible through our own strength, since we need the Holy Spirit himself (the particular help) in order to be able to forgive. We use and activate general help by asking God fervently and by persevering in our choice and with our request: we ask God to give us his Holy Spirit in order to become capable of forgiving the person who has offended us.

The Role of the Human Being in the Prayer of the Heart

The human being has a fundamental and decisive role to play in the Prayer of the Heart. God created the human being in his image and likeness; he created him with free will and with a capacity to love. The relationship between the human being and God, in the Prayer of the Heart, is a love relationship. St. Thérèse of the Child Jesus says: "to love is to give everything to God and to give ourselves to him." The Prayer of the Heart is an exchange of love in which God gives himself to us and we give ourselves to him. This exchange happens between two free wills. To this we need to add that the respect God has for the human being and for his freedom is absolute. God does not interfere in the area that belongs to the freedom of the human being. There is no doubt that God is all-powerful and can give orders, interfere with, and change things in the human being, but, in general, he does not do so. Since his very nature is love, he respects the human being's freedom, choices, and desires. This is why he does not interfere or give orders but, on the contrary, he invites, calls, awaits, exercises patience, and suffers.

Often we imagine God like a despotic emperor who does what he wants. This image of God is the product of our infirm imagination and has nothing to do with the reality of God. These are the reasons why we often reach great dryness in our relationship with God: we expect everything from him. In fact, he awaits our decision, choice, and action. In order to escape the trap of dryness and to allow the torrents of his grace to be unleashed, we need to understand more precisely our role. God constantly gives us his grace (general help) in order to ask for him, by offering ourselves to him. The role of the human being is fundamental as we need to use this constantly available grace. We must not lose time in formulating prayers and requests that have nothing to do with the real God Jesus has revealed to us.

✛

Since the intervention of the human being using the general grace of God is vital, it will not be sufficient to just "be in the presence of God" during prayer in order to be consumed by his fire. Let us examine this in detail. When the human being starts to pray he puts himself in the presence of God. This act is necessary since it sharpens his attention and opens the eye of his faith to see Jesus, who has risen from the dead and is present amongst us. If this act is prolonged a little more, the human being will become aware of the warmth of Jesus's love for him and he will become aware of Jesus's desire to pour the fire of his love into him. Despite that, we need to understand that putting ourselves in the presence of God is only the beginning of the path to prayer, not yet its core. There is still a substantial act to do, without which our heart cannot be enkindled by the fire of the Holy Spirit. Being in the presence of God resembles putting a flame at a short distance from a wick. Having no physical contact between the fire and the wick (Jesus and the human being's heart) does not lead to the wick being enkindled. What enkindles our heart with the fire of Jesus's love is *the act of offering of ourselves to him*, putting our life and our entire being in his hands. In this way, the human being plays his part entirely, through the grace of God.

This role that the human being plays evolves over time. When the human being becomes aware for the first time of the importance of his freedom and of how God waits at the door of his freedom to open to him (through the offering of all his being into the hands of God) and when the human being makes this act (of offering himself) for the first time, this will generate an outpouring of the Holy Spirit. The intensity of this outpouring is directly proportional to the completeness of the act of offering (complete, unconditional, like that of a little child). This outpouring is a new experience of God for the person. This experience reveals to him that, in true freedom and with the grace of God, he can receive the Gift of God.

The Role of Our Lady in the Prayer of the Heart

Mary's role in the salvation of humanity is as essential as is the role of a mother for her child. Without the mother, the child cannot be formed and does not grow. God wanted Mary to participate in his work of salvation and this does not contradict the fact that Jesus alone is the Savior. Jesus alone is God: this is why he alone is the Savior. But, out of excess of love, he does not want only to save us but he goes much further (and this is an amazing love!): he gives us a share in his work of the salvation of our brethren. St. Paul incarnates this when he says: "in my flesh I complete what is lacking in Christ's afflictions for the sake of his body, that is, the church" (Colossians 1:24). But Mary's role is far higher than our role in the application of Jesus's salvation of our brothers. On the cross, the first bride to come out of Jesus's side is Mary, the New Eve (see Genesis 2:21–23). Only after this do Jesus and Mary generate the whole Church, which means each one of us. The blessed Virgin is indeed truly the Mother of the Church. This is God's plan for humanity. On the cross, Jesus gives the New Eve as a mother to each one of us: "Behold, your mother" (John 19:27). We need then to meditate at length on Jesus's words about Mary's role in our spiritual life in the Scriptures and to imitate the beloved disciple, clearly allowing Mary a place in our heart: "And from that hour the disciple took her to his own home" (John 19:27).

The relationship between Jesus and Mary is unique. God created her and Jesus saved her—in anticipation—on the cross and made of her the pure and unique vessel that can contain his body in its heart: the God that "heaven and the highest heaven cannot contain" (1 Kings 8:27). Her creation before the birth of Jesus is not in contradiction with the fact that she has been saved by his blood on the cross. When the Son of God came into her womb she confessed and witnessed saying that he is her Savior: "my spirit rejoices in God my Savior" (Luke 1:47). There is only one Salvation, only one Savior, and the blessed Virgin, the New Eve, comes directly from Jesus's side on the cross. The cross is altogether in time and out of time (valid throughout all ages), and even if the Blessed Virgin brought forth Christ, she is his first fruit on the Cross.

Mary is "full of grace"; she is the only one who was capable of saying "yes" to the word of God at the Annunciation. Zechariah the Priest, who represents all the people of Israel, was not able to believe in the word of God (Luke 1:20). The blessed Virgin came after him and said "yes" for herself and for Zechariah, which means for herself and for all of us: we have, stored in her, our "capacity to believe." Truly, the gift of God is made of two parts: the Seed and the Earth; the whole (Jesus-God) and "the capacity to embrace the whole." God does not give us only Christ, the Divine-Seed, but he also gives us the capacity to receive the Seed and bear fruit as well. This capacity is deposited in the "Yes" that Mary uttered for us at the Annunciation and throughout her life.

We realize, then, two things: 1) the relationship between Mary and Jesus is unique and complete; 2) this relationship—of such immeasurable quality—is given to us.

The Blessed Virgin plays a fundamental role in our spiritual life, since she embodies for us the best way to follow Jesus. In the Scriptures, God shows the necessity of changing the heart of the human being from a heart of stone to a heart of flesh: "A new heart I will give you, and a new spirit I will put within you; and I will take out of your flesh the heart of stone and give you a heart of flesh" (Ezekiel 36:26). This new heart is made by Jesus on the Cross and is also called the "new man" (Ephesians 4:24) or the "new creation" (1 Corinthians 17:5). This new heart, like the "new skin" (Matthew 9:17), can contain the "new wine" that is the Holy Spirit (Ezekiel 36:26). This new heart, the heart of flesh, is not only in the image of the heart of Mary, but it is, to a degree, its own extension. It is generated by the action of the Holy Spirit in the heart of Mary our mother who from the very beginning said "yes" for each one of us. Nicodemus was correct when he asked Jesus: "How can a man be born when he is old? Can he enter a second time into his mother's womb and be born?" (John 3:4) John is using this question to make a strong allusion to something else. Truly, each Christian has to place himself within the heart of Our Lady, his real mold, where the Holy Spirit forms him in the likeness of Jesus, just as he formed Jesus himself in Mary's womb. To enter the spiritual life is to experience the Risen Lord. It is necessary for each Christian to imitate Mary at the moment of the Annunciation, asking God to give him a heart like hers where the Holy Spirit works with no obstacles.

The role of Our Lady in our spiritual life is constant. Her presence at our side and her direct action in our hearts are parts of the gift of God begun in baptism. The Christian faithful cannot doubt in any way that Our Lady is present at his side at all times. If the Christian does not see her with the eyes of his heart—the eyes of Faith—if he does not experience her presence, her care and intervention, the reason for this is not Mary; rather, it is his incomplete Christian formation. Whoever goes here and there in search of visions and apparitions, and forgets the presence of Our Lady beside him, in his house and in his work place, is content with the crumbs that fall from Jesus's table and does not try to find the substantial meal offered to him. This amounts to such sad ignorance.

There is an insistent desire and intercession on the part of Our Lady to help us to listen to Jesus's word and to put it into practice, so that he can dwell in us and us in him. Mary is a real mother who is ever watching over us; this is unquestionable. She waits for each one of us to give her total freedom of action, unconditionally and with no expectation of a return, so that she can do God's work, forming Jesus in us.

Often we start our prayers with our numerous requests and we forget that, according to the Lord, the "pagans" concern themselves with these things (see Matthew 6:32), and in doing the same we close the door to the work of God and Mary in us. This is why it seems to us that Our Lady does not act in our life. Therefore, we should invert our way of praying, giving God supremacy in everything, holding nothing back, since he said: "seek first his kingdom and his righteousness, and all these things shall be yours as well" (Matthew 6:33). He said *first* and he never added a second request, showing that it is necessary to concentrate all our energy on seeking God's will, putting him first in everything.

Above all else, we need to deepen our understanding of the place of Our Lady in Jesus's mission and her place in our life. This knowledge is necessary and opens up new horizons for us in our Christian life, giving it a new and powerful impetus. Mary's purity and perfection in her way of dealing with Christ are communicated to us step by step. Nobody can really evaluate the difference between having and not having recourse to our Lady, because the difference is of immense proportions. Before having recourse to Our Lady, when we go to Jesus directly, we rely on our own personal capacities. We cannot truly go to him directly, contrary to a common misunderstanding. The Holy Spirit cannot work freely in us. This is why the excuse of preferring to go directly to Jesus is a false excuse because going directly to him happens only through and in Our Lady. Through her and in her (that is, when we entrust ourselves to her) the Holy Spirit works in us with purity and perfection, linking us directly to Jesus. This knowledge (to know Mary and her role) compels us to entrust ourselves totally and unconditionally to God, placing ourselves in her hands, having total trust that thus the Holy Spirit can work in us in a perfect and efficient way.

Therefore, in order to attract Mary's action, we need to totally entrust ourselves to her care. The action of the Holy Spirit (in the field of entrusting ourselves) depends on the degree and quality of this entrustment. Mary takes what we offer her. If we choose not to entrust something in our life to her, she will not take it, and, as a consequence, she will not have the total freedom to act in us. For this, we need to cross the threshold of the door of grace in the proper way in order that God can pour out his abundant and pure grace on us.

If, during the day, we face some difficulties, obstacles, or problems, then it is necessary for us to entrust them to Mary, offering them to her with total trust and abandonment. Repeating these acts allows a rapid growth of the new man in us. This repeated entrustment is equivalent to pumping new blood into the baby (the new man) present in the womb of his mother, Mary.

✛

The general help and the particular help of the Holy Spirit have already been mentioned, and this intervention of Our Lady in our life and in our spiritual growth proceeds from the particular help of the Holy Spirit. On the cross, Our Lady comes out of Jesus's side, pure, the New Eve. This purity, the purity of the Bride ready for the Bridegroom, allows the action of the Holy Spirit to be perfect and without obstacles. This is why the angel called Mary "full of grace" (Luke 1:28). Jesus wanted Mary not only to be his mother but also the mother of his mystical body, that is, the mother of each one of us. The direct action of Our Lady in the human being cannot be separated from the work of the Holy Spirit. In fact, when we mention the Holy Spirit we mention Mary as well as she is the medium through whom and in whom the Holy Spirit works. When we speak of Mary we speak of the mother, our spiritual mother, and we in fact mention at the same time the Holy Spirit who works in her, in fullness.

The Prayer of the Heart is the act in which we offer ourselves to the Lord, where he takes us and puts us within himself and pours himself into us. The intervention of Jesus (his reception of our being, and the placing of us in him, and pouring himself into us) is the particular help of the Holy Spirit, which is also Mary's help. The three elements are in fact only one thing: Jesus's action = the action of the Holy Spirit = the action of the Holy Spirit in Mary.

The Characteristics of Mary's Help
We often invoke the Holy Spirit and Jesus but we forget to mention the Blessed Virgin's name. We forget to ask for her help. Since Jesus placed all his amazing mysteries in Mary and entrusted her with them, and since he has a great desire that we should discover her, and that through these discoveries we should discern new dimensions in him, we need to use divine intelligence and have recourse to

Mary. And we must do this repeatedly, at every moment of our lives, since there is no limit to the resources of Mary. Our love for her increases with our love for Jesus. The converse is equally true.

The characteristics of Mary's help are the following:

1) Ease: What is easier than for a baby to throw himself upon the bosom of his mother, knowing that she is constantly present at his side, taking care of him?

2) Certainty: Nobody has ever heard of anyone invoking Mary and being left unaided. She hastens to our help. Her coming is so certain that anything could be questioned except the fact of her immediate response.

3) Efficacy: The Holy Spirit acts in Mary in a perfect and total way. Therefore whatever she does to us is in fact done by the Holy Spirit.

4) Directness: God's action through Mary in us is a direct action with no intermediaries.

5) Purity: As we have said previously, the action of the Holy Spirit does not have any impurity or defect. When Our Lady acts, we can always be certain that this is the best and highest expression of God's will, because she acts in total purity according to the will of God. Her insight deeply penetrates the depth of God's will, intentions and desires; she chooses them and acts upon them.

6) Perfection: The fact that Mary's perfection resides in her capacity of containing Jesus-God in her, allows her to be the mold most capable of forming God's adoptive sons and daughters. God wants Mary to achieve her work in us with the same perfection.

7) Ensures Joy and Delight for Jesus: It is very difficult for the faithful to understand the relationship between Jesus and Mary in all its dimensions and depths. Therefore, it is difficult for us to evaluate the effect of Mary's actions on Jesus. But we can theologically deduce the influence of her acts on Jesus from their qualities.

8) Security: Since she preserves in her heart all the graces she receives, she continues that action in us by safeguarding the graces we receive.

Mary's role in the Prayer of the Heart is to gather and crystallize in her person all the necessary elements of the inner act of the Prayer of the Heart that make it successful. This is realized when the human being offers himself to God, like a baby, in the hands of Mary, so that she takes him and puts him into Jesus's furnace of love: his heart.

Humility is necessary in order to deal with God, for he is humility itself. Whoever makes himself like a little child realizes the essential part humility plays in our treatment of God. He who throws himself like a little child into Mary's arms realizes other necessary elements as well in order to make this connection with God successful: giving oneself totally, unconditionally, and surrendering with total trust. God's door is always open for Mary, because of Mary's capacity to keep the grace of God safe without losing it; and her knowledge of God's pure will aids in this, enabling thereby the interaction of the human being with God according to God's high and mysterious holiness and not according to our limited human vision. The fact is that Mary always comes, that is, she never delays in receiving us and placing us in God's being. All these elements are crystallized in Mary's being and in her action, and make her role in prayer fundamental and most especially in the Prayer of the Heart. Some saints say that we should not go to the Prayer of the Heart without Mary. In addition to this we can say, as a summary, that the Prayer of the Heart is Mary's personal domain and her preferred mode of prayer.

The Servants of the Prayer of the Heart

In the Church, within the Living Tradition—which is, along with the Bible, a fundamental element of Christian Revelation—we have the living tradition of prayer. This latter, like the Bible, is apostolic as well, which means that it is transmitted from generation to generation, from the time of the apostles. Jesus taught us to pray, and this living tradition of prayer is the stream that connects us to Jesus who is the *Orans* (pray-er) and the Master of prayer. The history of the Church is full of spiritual masters, who have been luminous signs down through the centuries. Jesus the Master poured on them special graces that allowed them to reflect the rays of his mastership of prayer. Each Christian—laity or priest—should draw from this living stream of the *Living Tradition of Prayer*. Each Christian, at a certain point in his life, in response to a special call from Jesus, may go to this stream in order to deepen the meaning of his baptism, striving to realize its goal: holiness. Jesus puts the stream of the living tradition of prayer into the heart of the Church in order to serve the development of the grace of baptism and the realization of holiness. The elements of this stream include: universities, theological institutions, monastic and religious orders, secular institutions, movements of the Church as well as other institutions within it. Even if these elements and their functions are different from the normal service in a parish, they serve the Church with humility and abnegation without interfering in the parish.

It is possible to summarize the three elements of the living tradition of prayer:

1) Persons who commit to holiness and live it; those who *experience* God in their depths.

2) A special *science*, the science of spiritual life, and of the experience of God, which is spiritual theology.

3) *Spiritual masters*, important luminous and living links who embody this stream and transmit its mysterious treasures to us, faithfully, with discernment, humility and authority.

It is important to notice that there is an uninterrupted, apostolic chain of masters of spiritual life which stretches through the centuries to the present time. This chain transmits spiritual life to us with the fire of the Prayer of the Heart and its specific discernment, generation after generation, from master to disciple. Discipleship here is necessary, just as the presence of a master is necessary. And, in turn, there is no master who was not first a disciple, and who received the living fire with discernment. The disciple will become like the master. This is why he should seek a real master. He needs to seek with prayer and fervent desire the one who acquired the fire in order to receive this immense and unique grace from God, that is, to have a good master. He who pretends to teach spiritual life and does not have the fire will have to pay God dearly for this. And, if he has acquired it, he needs to remain in it. Only after that is he allowed to speak and teach it. Whoever deviates from this line is described by Jesus as follows: "Truly, truly, I say to you, he who does not enter the sheepfold by the door but climbs in by another way, that man is a thief and a robber" (John 10:1). It is difficult for the human being to fully understand the Incarnation and its dimensions in all its depths. As St. John of the Cross says, Jesus has a great desire to come to us through a human master. It is the mysterious will of God not only to place his authority in the Church but also to go much further and place within her the authority of understanding, discernment, and spiritual direction. Whoever loves Jesus, will be introduced into his Heart; Jesus will teach him his will, and will show him that he earnestly desires to be reached through a spiritual master in order for discernment to be transmitted. The fact that the disciple will then follow the logic of Incarnation and its amazing humility, and will knock on the door of a master, makes Jesus open to him the abundant torrents of his grace, and give the faithful the seal of confirmation to his spiritual life.

He who chooses another way to receive Jesus's graces and to grow in spiritual life, disobeying the Incarnation's logic, simply errs. Soon he will sit with the devils, only pretending to have a spiritual life.

Part II: The Practice
of the Prayer of the Heart

In this second part we will learn how to practice the Prayer of the Heart. It is necessary to undergo this learning process. A greater part of Jesus's public life on earth was taken up in teaching us how to pray. The apostles acknowledged this when they said to Jesus, "Lord, teach us how to pray" (Luke 11:1). The human being is not born knowing how to pray. The grace of baptism does not absolve the faithful from learning to pray; on the contrary, learning how to pray is a condition for the seed of baptism to grow. Through baptism God deposits the Seed-Jesus in the human being, and invites him to take care of the seed until it reaches the fullness of its growth just as a good gardener would do. This care first and foremost constitutes prayer life.

How Do We Practice the Prayer of the Heart?

The Prayer of the Heart is an inner movement and the core of any prayer is to pray with the heart. Jesus reminds us of this: "when you pray, go into your room and shut the door and pray to your Father who is in secret" (Matthew 6:6). And the author of Romans encourages us to "offer yourself as a living sacrifice, holy and acceptable to God" (Romans 12:1). At Mass, the priest summarizes this in the invitation "Lift up your hearts." As we can see, the Prayer of the Heart is an inner act in which, with the help of the Holy Spirit, we move from where we are to God's Heart. This allows us then to truthfully answer "We lift them up to the Lord."

In Part I of this book, we addressed the different elements of this act. Now we will see them blended together into one single act. In this second part, we will study this act and its characteristics in order to learn how to practice it with ease.

✝

Let us now summarize the movement of the Prayer of the Heart:
First: I put myself in the presence of the Lord. It is better to be in

a quiet place in order to recollect my senses and thoughts and to be with Jesus-God present in my heart. I open the eyes of faith to see Jesus present, risen from the dead, and feel his desire to give himself to me. I may sign myself with the sign of the Cross and light a candle in front of the icon of Mary and the Child Jesus.

Second: I lift my heart to God. I offer myself totally, unconditionally, and irrevocably to Jesus in the hands of Mary, like a little child, with total trust and abandonment. Mary immediately takes me and puts me into Jesus's heart which is full of the fire of the Holy Spirit. The Holy Spirit acts in the depths of my heart, pouring himself into me, transforming me in him. Calmly, I keep repeating a short prayer that bears the name of Jesus and/or the name of Mary, whilst holding my rosary in my hands, following the natural rhythm of my breath. The prayer which I repeat silently expresses my desire and thirst for the fire of the love of Jesus.

Third: I repeat the act of lifting my heart, from time to time, according to need. Since it is possible to come out of Jesus's heart, I repeat the same act. I abide with him for the period of time that my spiritual director or master and I decided to allocate to this prayer.

Some Examples in Order to Understand the Movement of the Prayer of the Heart

The use of examples is important for our understanding of the movement of the Prayer of the Heart. In fact, in order for Jesus to introduce us to the inner world or the Kingdom, he used various parables as a spiritually efficient tool designed to unravel and explain the different aspects of the inner world and its laws. As Jesus said, he chose to use parables because "to you it has been given to know the secrets of the kingdom of heaven" (Matthew 13:11). The Prayer of the Heart is an inner movement that is invisible to the naked eye but is nonetheless a real act. In order for us to "see" it we need to adopt the language of parables and theological examples. The highest form of this language and the most simple and well-known one is the theological language of icons. The icon, with its lines, colors and symbols is an illustrative representation of words and theological meanings which help the human being, with the orthodoxy of its expressions, to connect directly with the mystery the icon painter or iconographer is contemplating (see below and the Appendix).

There are also simpler forms which God has put in front of us, and they speak to us about his mysteries: the parables of Nature. Nature, as St. Augustine said, is God's second book. St. Paul, quoting the Old Testament (Wisdom 13:3–5), affirms this: "Ever since the creation of the world his invisible nature, namely, his eternal power and deity, has been clearly perceived in the things that have been made" (Romans 1:20).

In the second part of this book we will use simple examples—diagrams—that will help us to understand the inner act of the Prayer of the Heart. Each example will address one of the theological angles of this act. At the same time, we need to appreciate the merit and the limitations of each example, since it is not possible to represent all aspects of the great mystery of the Prayer of the Heart.

First Example: *Example of the Sea*

The first diagram we use to describe the movement of the Prayer of the Heart is the diagram of the sea:

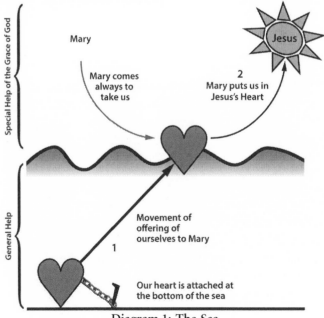

Diagram 1: The Sea

1) Our heart is at the bottom of the sea and wants to reach the inside of the sun which symbolizes Jesus's heart.

2) The distance between our heart and Jesus's heart is divided into two parts:
    a) The first part: moving through the water from the bottom of the sea to its surface.
    b) The second part: moving through the air and space, from the surface of the water to the inside of the sun.

What characterizes this diagram is that it incarnates many of the elements of the Prayer of the Heart and its movement. The bottom of the sea is a solid surface that symbolizes the hardness of our heart when it becomes a slave to a heavy sin or overwhelming anxieties. The water symbolizes our humanity, our emotions from which we should rise and give supremacy to Jesus above all else. Moving from the bottom of the sea to its surface symbolizes the offering of ourselves to Jesus the Lord, in a totally unconditional irreversible offering. The water represents the area of our freedom which God completely respects. He never dives into the water, violating our freedom; on the contrary, he respectfully waits at the "door," the border between our domain and his own. The air and space symbolize God's domain, "the Kingdom of Heaven." The master in this area, the area of space and sun (God's heart), and the one who controls the movement in it, is God alone and it is he alone who we need to hold in reverence. The admirable correlation between the symbols of this diagram and the theological elements of the movement of the Prayer of the Heart give this diagram a privileged place among the other examples we can use.

The movement of the Prayer of the Heart happens in the example of the sea as follows:

1) If we have any difficulty which paralyses us, we first need to present it to the Lord, putting it in his hands with total trust and abandonment.

2) We offer our heart to the Lord, in the hands of Mary, like a little child. In fact, this fundamental act moves our heart from the bottom of the sea to its surface where God awaits it. Offering ourselves to God is the key to the Prayer of the Heart.

3) Immediately when our heart reaches the surface of the water, God (or Mary) hasten to take it and place it in the sun: Jesus's heart full of the fire of love.

Moving in the "Water" and Moving in the "Air and Space"

In this example, the water refers to the general help, and the air and space refers to the particular help of the Holy Spirit as mentioned in the first part of the book. Therefore, we need to link these elements to the diagram of the sea. It is very important to understand the relationship between the freedom of the human being (always supported, of course, by the general help of the grace of God) symbolized by the water, and God's freedom, symbolized by air and space. The Prayer of the Heart consists in an encounter of love between God and the human being, where God respects the freedom of the human being, his will, and his personal space. In turn, from his perspective, the human being should understand the degree of respect God has for his freedom and that God waits for him to express his love freely, by giving himself to the Lord.

It often seems to the human being that God does not interfere in his life and does not act in his prayer, while, in reality, God is forced to a halt at the border (surface of the water) between the area of his freedom and the area of the human being's freedom, waiting for the latter to express his freedom by offering himself (using the general help). We need to fully comprehend that God never enters the water, since he does not want to invade the human being's freedom, or enforce him to make the act of oblation (act of offering).

It is true that God possesses everything, but he made a vow to himself that the human being would be in his image and likeness, would be free. In this sense, God does not own the human being's heart and would not dare to pour himself into him without an unambiguous expression of free will on the part of the human being.

The peerless way, both the highest and the purest, to make God pour himself into us is to place our heart in his hands, giving him total freedom to do what he wants with it. Jesus said that "men of violence take the Kingdom of heaven by force" (Matthew 11:12). According to God's language, when we surrender ourselves to him we paradoxically seduce him powerfully, and we start to "have power" over him, in the sense that when he sees something that is dear to him (our heart) in his hands he cannot but pour himself into us, since in his very nature he is like an unceasing torrent. For this reason, it is possible to use the verb "forcing" for God in this context, while this verb is not usually suitable for use in respect of his majesty.

When we cannot settle to prayer, first of all we need to understand that the spirit of prayer comes from above and that we need to be aware of it and ask for it. God is always the one who initiates the "circulation" of prayer.

It was mentioned above that, before starting to pray, it is possible that our heart is tethered to the bottom of the sea. This paralysis can happen to us at any time for various reasons; amongst them: a heavy sin, an overwhelming worry, a powerful event, and so forth. These factors have an influence over the performance of our will, as well as being capable of obstructing its interaction with the general help, which causes it to become paralyzed. The best way to overcome this obstacle and to be freed from it is to present it to God with total trust and abandonment, entrusting it to his hands. This act is always possible to us because of the general and constant help available through the grace of God; by availing ourselves of it we break the chain that ties our heart to the bottom of the sea, so that it frees our heart and we become ready to make the act of oblation.

This state of paralysis or this obstruction does not happen often; if it does, it happens more to beginners in the Prayer of the Heart. Since we can overcome this first obstacle (if it happens), and it is within our capabilities to practice the Prayer of the Heart at any time, there can be no excuses.

Some think that the presence of a heavy or grave sin can totally prevent us from being able to practice the Prayer of the Heart. This opinion is erroneous. Contrition is the destiny of any sinner, in the sense that before reaching Confession, there are no other routes other than *contrition*, which allows one to bemoan one's sin before God. But contrition itself also signifies a meeting with God, and a prayer made with our whole heart. How can a human being activate the grace of contrition if he does not—through contrition—present his sin to God, entrusting it to the hands of the Merciful God?

Of course this does not exempt us from confession, but it does show that the Prayer of the Heart is not only possible before confession but that it is necessary and imperative that we practice it in order for contrition to be formed in our heart.

The Conditions for a Successful Movement

The conditions for a successful movement are numerous. The act of offering should be open and without hesitation, sluggishness, rudeness, or arrogance. It should be imbued with humility; total and unconditional trust as well as irrevocable surrender. In making this act, we need to remember not to lean on our feelings, thoughts, imagination, or the desire to see what God is doing with us during prayer. When we decide to apply and use all these conditions, we find it quite difficult, if not almost impossible. Then we need a special grace from God which can crystallize and blend all these qualities into one. God gives us this Grace in the "yes" that Mary uttered in the name of each one of us. As we have seen, Mary plays a fundamental role in the Prayer of the Heart and in prayer in general.

If we offer ourselves, like small children, into the hands of Mary, she will always come to take and put us in Jesus's heart. In this way, all the conditions of the movement are fulfilled and crystallized in a higher and more efficient way. As God came down to man through Our Lady, so man goes up to God in the same way and with the same logic. The childlike offering of ourselves to Jesus, in the hands of Mary, is the secret of the saints and the state of holiness. Added to this, the meeting that occurs in Mary's arms between the human being and Jesus is a safe encounter, secure and perfect, because Mary's arms and womb are "full of grace" and only the Holy Spirit dwells in them and acts through them.

The Characteristics of the Act of Offering

In order for the act of offering to Mary to be good and efficient it has to be complete and without reserve. That is, we place our entire selves in her hands, not just a part of ourselves, such as emotions, passions, people, or anything we want to possess. Therefore, we need to avoid two types of bad offering as is shown below on the arrows of Diagram 2: The first arrow shows a sluggish, hesitant act of offering, not expressing our will and choice in an open manner. The act of offering shown by the second arrow has an excessive aggressiveness, rude arrogance, where we almost summon God to give himself in return for the gift of ourselves, as if it was something that was due to us and not a free grace resulting from God's love for us and from his sovereign freedom. The third type of offering is the correct one. The third arrow shows the best way of offering ourselves. It is clear, without reserve. On the one hand it is done without hesitation, and on the other there is no arrogant pride: it expresses our freedom in an unmitigated way, respecting God's freedom to give us his grace whilst at the same time having total trust in him and being able to surrender to him.

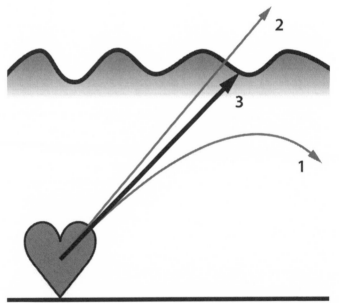

Diagram 2: The Three Arrows

The Prayer of the Heart is an encounter of love with Jesus who loves us and wants to pour the fire of his love into us and introduce us to the fire of his heart. To love is to give everything to Jesus and to give ourselves to him. Therefore, it is not possible to have this love exchange if we do not offer everything to him by placing it in his hands. This offering is also an act of detachment.

The Importance and the Place of the Act of Oblation in the Prayer of the Heart

We cannot stress enough that the act of oblation has a central place and is of vital importance. Offering oneself in order to accomplish the movement of the Prayer of the Heart is a step of paramount importance, since this offering (done with the simplicity of a child between the hands of Mary, without ulterior motives and with detachment) is what guarantees the success of the act of the Prayer of the Heart. "Success" means that a connection is really taking place in the depths of our being.

The presence and action of Mary are key to the constant success of the act of oblation. Once our hearts are given to her, she takes them immediately and immerses them in the fire of love of Jesus. She does this instantaneously, without keeping us for herself. She does it in a way that is efficacious and pleasing to Jesus. Why so? Because she is a real mother who knows the needs of our hearts, and the will of God—since she is guided by it—and is a worthy receptacle to *receive* our hearts.

If the beginner has some difficulty in making the act of oblation, it is important for him to have patience and to follow this teaching with complete humility and obedience, checking the fundamental practical points of that act until the act is crowned by success. When this act of offering is performed correctly, we receive the guarantee that a divinely intimate and authentic encounter will happen where God will unravel his treasures and the secrets of his love. There are some obstacles which the beginner must confront, such as distractions, lack of concentration, and these we will address later.

Second Example: *The Existential Example*

The second example which helps us to understand the Prayer of the Heart (see the diagram next page) shows the Prayer of the Heart as we perceive it and live it. It shows two areas of our awareness: (1) what happens in our mind/brain, symbolized by the square; (2) what occurs in our heart (in our chest), which is our "inner room" (Matthew 6:6) wherein God dwells. This diagram helps us to understand what occurs in us (mind, heart) when we are enacting the Prayer of the Heart and how we should interact with: (1) distractions; (2) the fact that we cannot sense God directly with our body and soul.

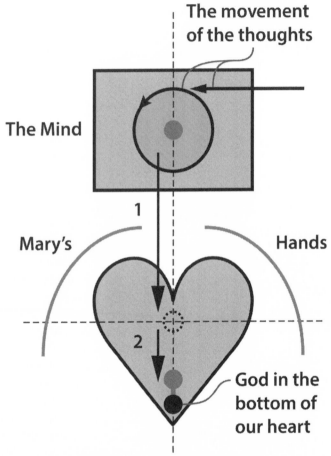

Diagram 3: An Existential Diagram

How does the Prayer of the Heart apply in this diagram? The act of offering—that is, moving from the bottom of the sea to the heart of the sun, passing through the surface of the water—is represented in this drawing as follows:

(1) One arrow moves from inside our thoughts (the square symbolizes the skull and the mind) to the frontier between man's free-

dom and God's freedom, at the entrance to the heart (see the horizontal hatched line, equivalent to the surface of the water on the drawing).

(2) A second arrow moves from the entrance of the heart to God who lives in its depths. Of course, the immense distance between the surface of the water and the sun is here symbolized by a very short distance between the heart and its depths.

Two arcs are added to the drawing: they protect the heart and the sacred encounter between God and us; they symbolize Mary's hands or her protection.

This diagram expresses our mobile presence in the following way. We notice in this diagram that we can move from one area of our being to another, and this can seem odd, since the mind, the senses, and the heart (the chest) do not move. So what does the following affirmation mean: *We moved and went down from the mind to the entrance of the heart, then to the center of the heart?*

First, the different use of the expression "heart" in both examples should not be confused. In the first example and in many situations we use the word "heart" to express our whole being. This is shown in the second diagram by a small circle which moves on the vertical axis (it has three positions on the axis). In the second example we use the word "heart" to allude to the chest, since God dwells in the center of our chest/heart.

Second, it is very important to know that a part of our being (the deep "I") can move. Science hardly speaks about this aspect and it is difficult to grasp since we associate our core being only with our consciousness or awareness. This wrong understanding introduces a great confusion in matters of prayer and meditation. One of the most common misconceptions is to believe that if we are distracted by our thoughts during prayer that this means that we have stopped praying. In fact what really happens in us is different from what we think: there is a difference between passive involuntary distraction and active voluntary distraction in which we are active in a truly willing way, through active thinking and/or imagining. Only active distraction can stop prayer from taking place, because when we follow our thoughts and produce more of them, our will and desire are diverted. This brings our core being out of the encounter with God.

Third, when we offer ourselves as a little child to Jesus, in the hands of Mary, in fact we come out of our brain/mind and reach our heart where, with the help of the Holy Spirit, we reach God. To go out from the brain/mind does not mean that we have disengaged the brain/mind or the senses or our consciousness (or that we have lost consciousness), but it does mean that our brain/mind has gone into a passive state. This is why Jesus said that the condition necessary to enter the Kingdom of God is to become like little children. The child's total trust and abandonment makes him go to his parents with his heart and not with his brain: he runs and throws himself into their arms. More precisely: there is in the child a direct, uncomplicated, and instantaneous line which leads from the brain/mind to the heart. When Jesus asks the adult to transform and become like a child (Matthew 18:3), he does not ask him to cancel the workings of his brain, but invites him to go directly to his heart (where God dwells) allowing God supremacy there.

Fourth, let us remember that because of its nature, the heart alone has the capacity to embrace God and to deal with him directly, while the mind does not have this capacity. Jesus does not invite the human being to "lose his mind" or his "consciousness," but, rather, he wants him to put each part of his being in its right place, and this means that the mind should return to its original inner room (Matthew 6:6), the heart.

To sum up, the act, by which we imitate the child, brings us (the core of our being) out of the box of our brain/mind to the area of our heart/chest. In this way, praying becomes an immersion of our being in Jesus's heart, and a dwelling in the chest where God is. If distractions arise while praying but we do not follow them, then there is good reason to believe that the core of our being remains immersed in God (in our heart). If we have any doubts, it is possible to repeat the offering of ourselves calmly.

Immersion in God does not disconnect us from our senses and from what they convey to us, nor it does not deprive us of our brain/awareness. Indeed, if anything happens in the senses or in the brain, it happens in a passive way. There is no contradiction in having both faculties operating at the same time: the immersion in Jesus on one side and the involuntary distraction on another. Prayer occurs in the heart where God pours himself into us directly and does not occur in the brain, since the very nature of God (uncreated) is much larger than the mind. We repeat: only the heart (our spirit, the core of our being) can enter into direct contact with God.

When we look at the two diagrams and at our movement in each one, we find that there is a discrepancy with regards to the direction of the movement of the core of our being. In the first example the movement ascends from below to *the greatest height*, on the face of it appearing to move outwardly from us to the Sun. While in the second example the movement goes from the mind to the depths of the heart, all of which takes place within us. Despite the apparent discrepancy, we find movement in both of them and this movement is the core of the Prayer of the Heart, since it embodies the offering of ourselves to God. The act of offering ourselves is a real movement which makes us come out of ourselves totally and throw ourselves into the hands of God. Expressing the movement can be made using different examples, in light of the fact that we are all unique, with varied needs and diverse ways of praying. One example may speak more to one particular category of person than another and, sometimes, different examples resonate in the same person, but in different phases of their spiritual growth. Since movement is at the core of the Prayer of the Heart, the discrepancy is only apparent, relating to the manner of expression and not to the content, since there is only one movement.

The Square and the Arrows
The square symbolizes the human brain/mind and, in a more physical way, the skull. When we pray, often we think that we (our "I") are one with our thoughts and mind. We think praying is thinking, saying things to God. Mostly, we think that, when we pray, if we get distracted in our thoughts, then we have stopped praying. Our conviction that "being distracted means that we and our brain are not with God" is a wrong one and we have to overcome it with a new conviction: that it is possible for us to be separated from our brain. We need to distinguish—in a categorical way—between the thoughts that are present in our brain/mind and the place where we are. This means that these two operations can take place simulta-

neously: (1) the presence of thoughts, rambling around in our brain/mind in a passive involuntary way; (2) being present in the depths of our heart, with God, in prayer. Thus, it is absolutely possible to be with God, united with him in prayer, in our depths, and at the same time not to be present in the "square" of the brain/mind. Being present with God in our heart (in the chest, which is the place of prayer) does not eradicate the passive action of our senses and brain. While praying we do not lose consciousness (that would be an *ecstasy*); we remain quietly aware of what is happening around us and of the presence of involuntary thoughts in our mind. If we do not attach importance to what is happening around us, we can remain in faithful contact with God in our depths.

On the diagram of the second example we find two types of arrows in the brain:

1) an arrow which enters the square from the outside. This symbolizes the thoughts that come to us from outside (no matter what the source), and which can distract us;

2) a round arrow, inside the square of the brain, symbolizing the thoughts that come from our memory to which we should pay no attention.

Obviously, as we said previously, we should not give importance to these thoughts and if they occur and we start to deal with them in an active way, we will most probably come out of the immersion in God. When we become aware of our active distraction, we should quietly repeat the act of offering of ourselves to God, in order to become immersed in him through prayer once again.

The Heart and the Arcs

In the second diagram, the heart symbolizes the chest of the human being, where God dwells. As they appear physically as part of the human being's structure, there is a difference between the skull and the chest. This difference as expressed in the drawing helps us to distinguish, in a radical way, between what occurs in the human mind and chest during prayer. God, with whom we want to be united, is not in the brain, since it is too limited and therefore cannot contain God's being, while the chest of the human being and his heart are created by God, and are thus capable of "containing" him and dealing directly with him, without any intermediary. This distinction makes the human being, the seeker of God, seek him in his heart and not in his mind.

The two arcs above the right and on the left of the heart express the protection of Our Lady and the necessity of asking for her aid. It is important to explain the role of Mary in preserving this encounter and protecting it.

Our Lady's Role

After offering our heart to Jesus, in the hands of Our Lady, it is preferable to repeat a short sentence, according to the natural rhythm of our breathing, in silence, holding our rosary in our hands. It is desirable to have Jesus's and/or Mary's name in this short sentence/ prayer, since repeating the name resonates with a deep spiritual echo: it does not only call the person but it also attracts the work of this person. Jesus's mission is to enact his salvation (the name "Jesus" means "God saves"), while Mary's is to exercise her all-powerful intercession. One of the meanings of "Mary" is "star": she is the one who perfectly reflects Jesus's light. Star of the Morning— another of Mary's names—designates the one who leads us in the darkness and prepares us for the dawn: Jesus. This repetitive prayer has two effects. The first one, through expressing our desire, is to keep alight the fire of the encounter. The second effect is that while calling for the help of Our Lady, we receive her protection in the encounter between God and ourselves. In the drawing, the two arcs symbolize the hands of Mary, as if she were supporting our heart in order to give her protection to the encounter. We should not forget that human and divine nature met and were united in Mary's heart and womb. God maintains the same logic and makes of Mary the place where the encounter between us and Jesus happens in the Holy Spirit.

It is important to clarify that the place where the encounter with Jesus happens during the Prayer of the Heart (in Jesus's Heart) is enveloped by Mary in her luminous mantle, or in her womb, or in her heart. As was the case with Christ-the-Head (the union between divine and human nature in Mary's heart and in her womb), it is the same for Christ-the-Body: the encounter between us and Jesus happens in her womb. God does not change his logic. What if, because of our weakness, we come out of the encounter? First and foremost, God does not look at the length of an uninterrupted encounter; rather, he looks at the degree of our trust in him and the quality of our offering when we offer ourselves to him repeatedly. For various reasons (for example, our weakness) we often come out of the encounter. Frequently distractions have an influence on us. The thoughts and the images present in our mind and in our imagination, cease to be involuntary and become voluntary. This happens when they hold sway over us, as we start to accept them, activate them, and persevere at length with them. Thought and imagination have a great influence, especially over the beginner: he cannot easily neglect or forget them. In reality, they fulfill no purpose, whether passive or active.

We can compare thoughts and imagination to a ferocious wolf wanting to devour us. Our fear and terror of this wolf prevent us from seeing the strong chain attached to him, preventing him from getting closer to us, keeping us safe. It would be good to learn from this example: to remain calm and still, not being concerned about anything that happens in our mind or in our imagination during the Prayer of the Heart. What our mind and our imagination see does not have any existence in the reality of prayer as is the case in a movie. For instance, if a murder occurs in a movie, this does not mean that the actor actually died in real life, or that we took part in the murder.

When, because of our weakness, we come out of the encounter we need to react calmly, not getting angry with ourselves because this will create a useless battle inside us; a war that is a sign of our lack of humility and of acceptance of our weakness. We should repeat the act of offering of ourselves to the Lord: he will respond again and put us in his heart again. God is not surprised by our weakness, and he does not blame us for it, but awaits yet again our offering of total trust in him.

We should not forget that the Prayer of the Heart is a relationship founded on love, and that the tie between us and God is the fire of that love, the fire of the Holy Spirit.

Third Example: *Praying before an Icon*

First and foremost whoever wants to understand the meaning of an icon and its benefits in our spiritual life should read the "Appendix," at the end of this book.

The icon is a unique grace which Jesus gives us in order to help us recollect our thoughts and put ourselves in front of one of his mysteries and, through it, enter the state of prayer. The icon is a consequence of the Incarnation: it takes our weakness into consideration, supporting and strengthening it. It is wise and an act of humility, for our part, to use the icon in order to enter the state of prayer and to avoid distractions as much as possible. Truly, the icon facilitates the Prayer of the Heart enormously, since it draws us toward the mystery depicted on it, and almost engulfs us in it, thanks to the grace associated with it. Indeed, the Church blesses each icon for use in worship. From that moment onwards, a grace accompanies it, a grace which helps each of the faithful in his prayer to enter the mystery of God depicted in that icon.

The most widespread icon is the Madonna and Child for the simple reason that it most closely reflects what happens in the depths of our heart. Our soul is unable to witness our encounter with Jesus-God as it happens in our spirit. What the eyes of the body and soul cannot see, the icon depicts in clear theological lines. With theological faithfulness, the icon expresses the mystery of what is happening in us, i.e., the mystery of our meeting with Jesus, without taking away or diminishing any dimension of the mystery. On this icon, Mary embodies the perfect disciple and, at the same time, draws us toward this goal: in her and with her we are empowered to worship perfectly, "in Spirit and in Truth."

Fourth Example: *The Anthropological Example*

At the beginning of this book we mentioned the existence of the soul and the spirit of the human being, and we compared them to a high mountain. In the following diagram we express in a simple way the soul and the heart (the spirit) and God. As we can see, the heart falls between the conscious soul and God. Since God is the inner center of the human being, we have portrayed him as a dot (like the center of a circle in geometry). The closest part of the human being to God is his heart: it is the most sublime part of him. The heart is the "image and likeness" (Genesis 1:26) of God in us.

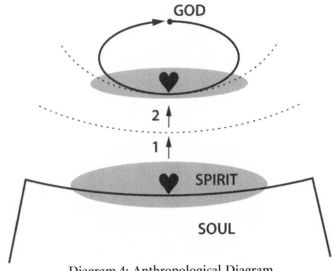

Diagram 4: Anthropological Diagram

The Veil between the Soul and the Spirit

As we can see in Diagram 4, there is a veil between the soul and the spirit. This means that there is a difference between the fabric of the soul and that of the spirit. As we have said previously, the soul and the body comprise the conscious part of the human being. Its capacity does not allow it to enter into direct contact with God. All that it receives from God—in this life and in the following—is only a created echo of God himself. This echo is like crumbs that fall from the substantial banquet God prepares for the spirit, that is, himself. The nature of the fabric of the spirit allows it to be touched directly by God. According to the Fathers of the Church, the spirit of the human being, is the very "image and likeness" of God. After the Fall, we lost the "likeness," and the Holy Spirit is re-forming it in us. The existing difference between the fabric of the spirit and the fabric of the soul creates the semblance of a barrier between the two, expressed here by the veil. God's light that passes from the spirit to the soul is not only refracted (like a light ray that travels from air through water) but changes in nature: from an uncreated nature (the very nature of the Creator) to a created grace.

The passing or not of any grace to the soul and to the body is something which is totally dependent on God's wisdom, since this passing is not of itself necessary for our sanctification. By "passing" we mean the presence of a feeling or sensing in the soul and/or the body. These feelings and sensations are echoes of the principal grace of God given in the spirit. The degree or intensity of the feeling (soul) or the sensing (body) of the grace of God is variable; only the wisdom of God sees it and operates it.

In the early stages of spiritual growth, the soul and the body are not pure, and the way they operate is still in the manner of the "old man" (or "old creature"). God will not pamper one with consolations, because one can become attached to them and idolize them. The "old man" tends to go to God not for himself but for the consolations the seeker receives. Such a motivation is impure and the seeker is in need of the grace of discernment in order to detect and remove it.

God

As we can see in the diagram, God is depicted by a small dot. It is not wrong to portray him thus because Jesus already symbolizes the Kingdom of God—God in us—with the tiniest seed: "It is like a grain of mustard seed, [...] the smallest of all the seeds on earth" (Mark 4:31). God is the center of our life and he is not only present everywhere but, through baptism, he dwells in the depths of our heart. We have a heaven in our heart, says St. Teresa of Avila. She adds, in the same vein, that since he is in our heart, Jesus is very close to us and that we do not need to shout loudly in order to be heard and to enter into contact with him. Our quiet voice and our thoughts are all before him. We can say that, in the diagram of the sea, the immense distance between the surface of the water and the sun is actually very much reduced in this diagram, amounting to no more than a few centimeters. Truly God is close to us, but we cannot enter his depths without his grace. As is the case in the example of the sea, there is a point of contact between water and air—

between our freedom and God's. Likewise, in this diagram there is a point of contact we cannot cross with our own strength (see the hashed line, Diagram 5). It is important to notice that the dot that symbolizes God is in dark black, which alludes to a great intensity— God's divine nature—from which the Holy Spirit emanates and operates in us when we pray.

Applying the Diagram to Us

The diagram expresses the movement of the Prayer of the Heart anthropologically as follows. The Prayer of the Heart is about elevating our heart to God, who comes and takes our heart, placing it within his heart. As we saw in the preceding diagram (Diagram 4), during the movement of offering, our heart can be in three different places on the same axis:

a) The heart is in its original position, inside the space of our freedom, close to the soul.

b) By offering ourselves (arrow 1), the heart reaches the contact line between our freedom and God's action (hashed line).

c) When God takes our heart and places it in himself, he elevates it (arrow 2) and brings it closer to him and pours himself into it.

Fifth Example: *The Circles of Freedom*

This fifth diagram is composed of two half-circles meeting at one point. We find on it as well two small circles in black: one (a) is at the center of the first half circle, and the other one (b) is at the junction between the two half circles. God (b) is standing at the door of our freedom, waiting for us to come to him, to open the door to him, and offer ourselves to him. We (a) move (arrow) from the center of our freedom (center of the half-circle) to the contact point with God.

As we can see in the diagram (next page), there is no interference between our freedom and that of God. God never forces us to give ourselves to him, nor does he violate our freedom. He does not enter our space. He created us in his image and likeness, which means that we are free, capable of loving (giving ourselves) or of not loving. Likewise, we cannot enter God's domain, force him or violate his space. The language of love is the language of freedom, the language of the gift of ourselves in total freedom. God wants to give himself to us unconditionally, unceasingly, constantly, but he never imposes himself on us. He respects our freedom and waits for us to give ourselves to him, this is why he says, "Behold, I stand at the door and knock; if any one hears my voice and opens the door, I will come in to him and eat with Him, and He with me" (Revelation 3:20). This is why the door handle is plainly on our side, which means that our freedom is in our own hands.

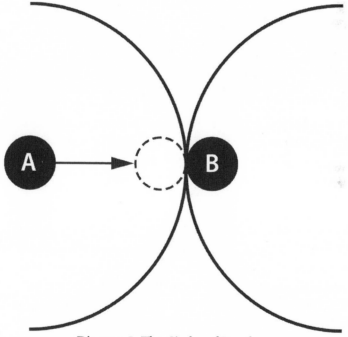

Diagram 5: The Circles of Freedom

In order to understand this example and the necessity to move toward God in order to establish the contact and union, we need to remember what we do when we shake hands with somebody: each one of us extends his hand toward the other, toward an invisible middle point between the two of us. Nobody extends his hand further than this point trying to snatch the other one's hand; on the contrary, we wait prudently and watch the movement of the hand of the other person, waiting for a movement which expresses the decision of the other person and his or her choice. The same happens for the Prayer of the Heart with the difference that God's hand is constantly extended, reaching the meeting point, and waiting for us to extend our hands to him.

Sixth Example: *Praying at Home with Children*

What Happens in the Mind and What Happens in the Heart

The following is a very simple example to help us deal with distractions. We know perfectly well that we cannot eradicate distractions from our conscious mind, since our senses work unceasingly and allow a considerable amount of interference to come in. The encounter with God happens elsewhere: in our heart/our chest, and not in our mind.

Let us take an example in order to understand to what extent we are free and independent of what is happening in our heart in the face of the distractions and noise which happen in our minds: let us imagine that the mind and the chest are like the two floors of one house. On the second floor (the floor of the mind) there are young children making a good deal of noise playing, and we are on the first floor (the floor of our chest) trying to pray. In general, it is not possible to control the children and calm them down, but as we have to live with this "noise," it is possible to shut the staircase door and get on with our prayer. This will not totally cancel the noise coming from upstairs, but it will diminish its influence on us.

This example shows us the existence in us of two distinct floors and that there is no physical interference between the area of the brain and that of the chest (or the heart). God is present on the first floor, we are present with him, and there is nothing capable of preventing us from having direct contact with him. This example, if we visualize it with great care, will liberate us to a great extent from the influence of the distractions, and will ease our communication with God. We will understand the coexistence in the same house of two different things: the noise upstairs and the quiet Presence of God downstairs. Whilst we cannot put a stop to the children, we can lessen their influence on us.

The only thing left to our freedom is to acknowledge the existence of the door between the two floors, and to close it. This happens when we repeat quietly, with the natural rhythm of our breath, a short prayer invoking Our Lady's help. Her presence and her protection do not eradicate the noise completely, but it diminishes it considerably, and gives the encounter with God and the immersion in him a greater chance to last longer.

Seventh Example: *The Fire and the Wick*

God is a "devouring Fire" (Deuteronomy 4:24) who needs to ignite our heart, but he cannot enkindle our heart with his fire if we do not offer it to him totally, putting it in his hands with complete abandonment, leaving to him—with total trust—all the freedom to act in it as he desires and to engulf it as he wants. This condition looks like the required condition to kindle a wick: it has to be dry. If the human being does not present himself with complete abandonment to God, he resembles a wet wick, and the fire cannot take hold. But, once the wick is dry (offering ourselves totally), the fire will take immediately. We understand from this, once again, how much God respects our freedom and his desire not to overlook our freedom. At the same time, this example introduces us further into the depths of God's "bowels of Mercy" (Luke 1:78), allowing us to discover—since he is a devouring fire—the extent of his thirst (see John 19:28) for us and how much he is attracted by us—out of love.

Whoever wants to understand God's desire to love him, let him put a tuft of wool or hair close to a candle's flame and witness the speed with which the fire will take hold: this will give him an idea of how God pursues us, and devours our heart with the fire of his love for us once we offer it to him. God's fire does not harm the human being when it invades him; on the contrary, it purifies him, taking away from him all that is not God. God's fire is a fire of love.

Eighth Example: *Longing and Yearning*

What are the roles of desire and sighs in the Prayer of the Heart? Commenting on the Psalms, St. Augustine writes several times that prayer can be summarized by our desire and yearning: "that very desire of your heart is your prayer." This is common in the Bible: "As a hart longs for flowing streams, so longs my soul for thee, O God. My soul thirsts for God, for the living God" (Psalm 42:1–2). It is important to notice that the desire is a real interior act that makes us come out of ourselves with a strong thirst, searching for God, our Beloved. Sometimes this inner act is initiated when we express to God, with simple and spontaneous expressions, our desire for him. In such a case, the act and the words are simultaneous and combined; the words carry the act and make it happen. They embody it.

This reality shows us two things: 1) words and acts are different; 2) it is possible to exercise ourselves in inner acts of desire without necessarily saying words. It is important to pay attention to the type and the intensity of the acts of longing. Desiring God is a real act of thirst, like a mouth open, full of fire and heat and thirst, in a terrible desert, under a midday sun, longing for some water. To the same degree in which this act is accomplished, God reacts to us giving us himself.

St. Teresa of Avila, teaching us the Prayer of the Heart, repeats on several occasions that looking at Jesus is fundamental and that we should not take our eyes away from him. It is possible to overlook this advice, but in this case we would lose a very powerful tool in the practice of the Prayer of the Heart. In order to properly evaluate this advice, we need to remember that she often mentions Jesus's beauty. Beauty in itself attracts. In our fallen nature, beauty can and often does trigger fantasy and carnal desire, or simply human longing. Staring at length at something beautiful or a beautiful being brings it closer in some way, so that our desire for it is enhanced. Jesus is God, the Eternal Son Incarnate; he is very beautiful in his Glory and in his Passion. Therefore, let us never take away our eyes from him, so gazing at him becomes a new habit in us that will generate a desire and a longing; let us also express our desire for him in various ways and acts. In this context, St. Teresa of Avila reminds us of a very powerful truth capable of increasing the fire of our love for Jesus: from the excess of his love for us, he never takes away his eyes from us! Who is this Jesus? Who are we in your eyes, for you to love us to such an extent? Who are you to love us in this way? Let us ask Our Lady to give us a heart like hers, so that it will be inflamed by the love of the Bride for the Bridegroom.

Ninth Example: *The Example of the Inner Room*

In the Sermon of the Mount, Christ taught us to pray, saying "when you pray, go into your room and shut the door and pray to your Father who is in secret" (Matthew 6:6). This explanation is very precise and we need to understand it in order to practice it. In fact, it is totally in accordance with the Prayer of the Heart and aptly describes it. In order to understand it we will use a diagram.

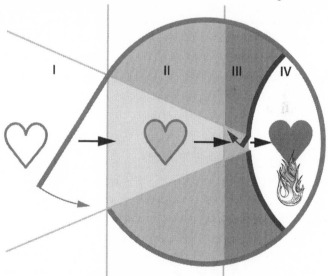

Diagram 6: The Inner Room

In this diagram we see all the elements of Jesus's words. The big circle that has an exterior door open to the left represents our "room," that is, our conscience. This big door is the door of the senses that connects us with the external world (area I). Inside our room we see three different areas: II, III and IV. The first and largest area is II, which represents our conscience in general terms. This is the place where we enter when we want to think, meditate, examine our conscience, or just want to be with ourselves. It signifies *entering into ourselves*, inwardly withdrawing to the area where man is alone with himself. Entering this area is accessible to any person, with the general help of the grace of God.

After entering our room, Jesus invites us to "shut the door" which means that we need to change our interests from the outside world and from creatures and bring ourselves toward God dwelling inside our room. This is an act of recollection, or "prayer of recollection" as St. Teresa of Avila teaches it. The area IV is a sacred space in us where God himself lives, depicted by a flame in the diagram. We cannot enter this area, the Kingdom of God, without the particular help of the Holy Spirit. This is why Jesus invites us in his explanation (Matthew 6:6) to "pray to your Father" which means to ask and beg the Father to allow us in where he is, and to "knock" at the door of the Kingdom. Area III expresses this "begging," which, if made from the heart, is equivalent to an offering of ourselves. It corresponds, in the diagram of the sea, to the arrow through which we move from the bottom of the sea to the surface. This area (III) does not express a place where we dwell but rather it is the sign of an impulse and momentum which occur when we ask with insistence. We see in this diagram how it is possible to be inside our conscience in three different places, depending on our desire and personal decision.

With this understanding we can acknowledge how the previous explanation of the Prayer of the Heart complies with Jesus's explanation of how we should pray in Matthew 6:6.

Our Place in Prayer

In all religions, there is always a special place dedicated to worship, where God is present in a more intense way than usual, or a direction towards which one should turn to worship. For instance, in the Old Testament God used to dwell in the Temple in Jerusalem, in a place called "the Holy of Holies." As a consequence, prayer, worship and sacrifices used to be made in the presence of God in the Temple. Those who did not live in Jerusalem and needed to pray or to seek the Lord's help, had to face Jerusalem's mountain. The Samaritans worshipped on another mountain.

When the Eternal Son became Incarnate, he revolutionized worship. He made us understand that he is the true temple where God lives, and that the Jerusalem temple was only a pale figure of the true temple: himself. The revolution in worship introduced by Jesus did not erase the human physical side of it (we still gather in churches) but it opened a new space for worship and prayer: Jesus himself, who is sitting at the right hand of the Father.

Let us hear again Jesus's revolutionary words to the Samaritan lady: "Woman, believe me, the hour is coming when neither on this mountain nor in Jerusalem will you worship the Father. [...] But the hour is coming, and now is, when the true worshipers will worship the Father in spirit and truth, for such the Father seeks to worship him. God is spirit, and those who worship him must worship in spirit and truth" (John 4:21; 23–24). We understand from this new teaching that our place in prayer is in Jesus himself (who is the Truth) and that prayer happens really only through the Holy Spirit.

Our Place in the Trinity

With the Incarnation of the Eternal Son and with the salvation he realized on the cross, God prepared for each one of us a place in Jesus's Mystical Body: "In my Father's House [my Body] are many rooms [...] And when I go and prepare a place for you [on the cross], I will come again [through prayer] and will take you to myself, that where I am [at the right hand of the Father] you may be also [while on earth]" (John 14:2–3). Let us remember as well that, from the time of our baptism, we are Jesus's Body (see John 2:21, 1 Corinthians 12:27).

Through baptism we are immersed in the Trinity, open to the life and being of the Trinity. When we pray and worship our place is as follows: we are

before the Father,
in the Son Incarnate,
through the Holy Spirit.

In fact, on the cross, Jesus opened the *way* (see the "new way" in Hebrews 9:8; 10:20) for us to communicate with the Father because being in the Son gives us direct access to the Father. By dwelling in the Son, there are no obstacles or distances between us and the Father.

When we pray the Prayer of the Heart, we present ourselves to the Son, who embraces us in his arms (the Holy Spirit and the Blessed Virgin Mary) and introduces us into himself. By being in the Son, we are therefore in the Trinity, participating in the life of the Trinity (see 2 Peter 1:4), in front of the Father, with the Holy Spirit. Dwelling in the Son makes him pour his Holy Spirit into us, transforming us in Christ.

In the following diagram, we see how our body dwells in Jesus's body, our soul in his soul, and our spirit in his spirit. This is our place during the Prayer of the Heart.

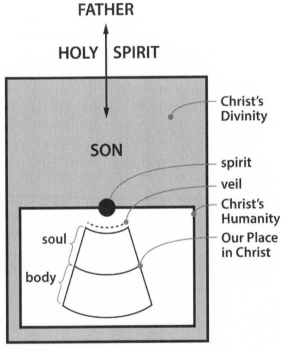

The Son Incarnate
Our Temple
Diagram 7: Our Place in the Son

Our Place in Jesus's Name

In St. John's Gospel Jesus says, "whatever you ask in my Name, I will do it" (John 14:13). This is a clear invitation to us from Jesus that when we pray we should always ask the Father "in Jesus's Name." However, we need to understand the deep significance of this invitation in order to put it into practice.

In the Old Testament, God revealed his Holy Name to Moses (Exodus 3:15): YaHWeH. He described himself to Moses as a "devouring fire" (Deuteronomy 4:24). He even wanted to show him his nature as a devouring fire in the event of the burning bush (Exodus 3:2–3): a fire that burns but does not consume. The fire of love kindled in the heart of the human being burns his whole being but never destroys or annihilates him.

God is fire, and the Second Person—whose nature is fire—took flesh. God's name, YaHWeH came closer to us and became YeShua (Matthew 1:21). YeShua is a verb, an action, which means: "God (YeH) saves (Shua)" (Matthew 1:21). Jesus's name alludes to the constant action of God saving us. But what does "to save us" mean? Jesus on the cross saves us: he delivers us from "outer darkness" (Matthew 22:13) to God's Being: the fire. This is how the fire saves us: he transforms us into him, bringing us into the depths of his inner life.

This means that each time we pray, we need to be *in* Jesus's Name, inflamed by his fire, under the influence of the *action* of his holy Name; in another words, when we pray, we are dwelling in Jesus ("in Jesus's Name") calling on God the Father.

During the Prayer of the Heart we say "Jesus," calling to him for his salvific work, asking him to draw us into himself, drawing us (saving us) into the devouring fire of his love. If we pray in his Name (being in him), God always answers our prayer. In fact, we ask from God-the-Fire to give us his fire. When we invoke the Name of Jesus, we place ourselves in him, so it is as if the fire (Jesus in us) is asking fire (the Holy Spirit) from the fire (the Father).

Our Place in Our Lady

When we mentioned above the role of Our Lady in the Prayer of the Heart, we saw how Jesus, being at once perfect God and perfect man qualifies him as everything for us and makes him our temple. We saw how the Blessed Virgin is not only the best disciple who followed Jesus, but she is also the mother of whoever follows him. Our being rebuilt as a "new man" in Christ is indeed a great mystery. An equal mystery is having Mary as our mother and the "womb" where are formed by the Holy Spirit. As St. Augustine says, all those predestined, while in the world, are hidden in the womb of the Blessed Virgin where they are protected, nourished, cared for, and developed until the day she brings them forth to a life of glory after death. Our Lady is from Jesus and remains in him; therefore, whoever is in her womb is also in Christ.

In a simpler way, we can say that during prayer we are not only in Christ, before the Father but we are also in Mary before Jesus. This is why we said that the movement of the Prayer of the Heart is an offering of ourselves in the hands of Mary. St. Thérèse, likewise, abandons her offering to Our Lady.

The following diagram (next page) is an attempt to draw the relationship between Jesus and Mary in the Holy Spirit. Jesus, our God and sun, is represented by a circle (the traditional symbol of infinity), and Mary, who reflects Jesus's light in all purity and who is capable of embracing Jesus-God in her bosom, is represented by the moon. The Holy Spirit is the "bond" (Colossians 3:14) of love between them. Thus we understand the two parts of faith: 1) the objective part, Jesus-God, who is the center of our faith; and 2) the subjective part, Mary, the embodiment of the perfect believer, and the mother of all believers. This diagram shows us our place while praying: we are within our Mother, in front of Jesus, in the Holy Spirit.

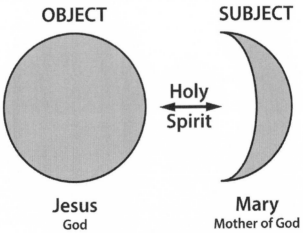

Diagram 8: Jesus and Mary

The Summary of the Prayer of the Heart

We can summarize the Prayer of the Heart in the following three steps. The first step is not mandatory and the third one repeats the second.

First: Preparation (not mandatory)

— Signing ourselves with the sign of the cross

— Putting ourselves in the presence of God and Our Lady (for instance: lighting a candle in front of an icon of the Mother of God).

— Invoking the Holy Spirit, the fire of God's love, the core of any movement of admittance into God's presence.

— Unconditionally abandoning and emptying all our burdens into Jesus's hands: all that is good and bad in us, throwing everything into the fire of his love (do briefly).

Second: The Movement of Immersion in God

Interiorly

— Offering ourselves: we offer ourselves to God, like little children, in the hands of Our Lady.

We keep our inner eyes (imagination and thoughts) closed, without activating them, i.e., wanting to see what God does)

— God's response: Mary always comes at once, taking us and immersing us in the furnace of love, Jesus. During this immersion, God gives himself to us, pouring his Spirit into us.

Exteriorly

— We hold our rosary in our hands (optional, but highly recommended).

— With each bead we peacefully and silently repeat the "Hail Mary" or any other short prayer that contains Jesus's name and/or Mary's.

— We repeat this prayer quietly, according to our natural breathing rhythm.

Third: Repeating the Movement of Offering

— Peacefully, we repeat the movement of offering ourselves from time to time, according to our need and to the presence of distractions, because it often occurs that we come out repeatedly from this immersion.

— We persevere in the repetition for the time we have decided to give to God. (We can be aware of the time that passes by checking the time occasionally.)

Part III: Other Concerns about the Prayer of the Heart

In the first part of the book we addressed the different components of the act of the Prayer of the Heart. In the second part we watched the act being performed and described it under various angles and diagrams in order to grasp its essence. Now, this third Part is divided in two sections. The first one will address various practical questions around the Prayer of the Heart. In the second section we will see different aspects of the relationship between the Prayer of the Heart and the life of the Church.

PRACTICAL QUESTIONS

✝

The Prayer of the Heart and Time

How much time do we need to dedicate to the Prayer of the Heart? It is important to dedicate a period of time daily to the Prayer of the Heart. This time is equivalent to a substantial and necessary meal, because the Prayer of the Heart is a great source of food for the hours that follow it; this is what we ask of God on a daily basis: "give us this day our daily bread." It is vital and healthy to have at least two meals per day, one in the morning and the other in the evening.

The beginner should start with 10 or 15 minutes in the morning and the same in the evening and persevere for a month or two, according to need. After that, he can increase to 20 or 25 minutes, and should persevere again for a month or two.

If the practitioner is generous and practices *lectio divina* daily, he will be able to increase the time of the Prayer of the Heart, progressively from 20 to 60 minutes at a time. Obviously, anyone who practices the Prayer of the Heart to such an extent should seek spiritual direction to allow God to confirm him in his spiritual journey, giving him discernment, firmness and fruitfulness.

✝

How do we spend our time during the Prayer of the Heart? After we have taken the resolution to dedicate some time morning and evening on a daily basis to the Prayer of the Heart, we then find that we have a period of time (10 minutes, 20 minutes, etc.) at our disposal which we have to manage and dedicate in the best way possible. We should endeavor to spend it, in so far as we are able, in *real* inner contact with God, where he pours himself into us. As the encounter happens in our spirit (the supra-conscious part of ourselves), it is not possible to discern whether the encounter is really happening or not. Therefore, as we said before, during this time, we need first and foremost to practice the act of offering ourselves, and, from time to time (whether we are in contact or not), to repeat it. In the event that we were not in contact with God, this will be re-established; otherwise, we will continue to remain in God.

In order to maintain consistency in having real contact with God, and to diminish the influence of distractions on us, we need to hold our rosary in our hands and repeat with great desire and thirst our love for Jesus and Mary.

If we are actively distracted, that is, if we take part in the distraction (active distraction), whenever we become aware of it, calmly, and without becoming upset with ourselves, we need to accept our weakness and address it by repeating anew our act of offering. We are not invited to practice the Prayer of the Heart during the allocated times only; on the contrary, we should strive to practice it often during the day, renewing our act of offering at any time and in any circumstance, because nothing can stop us from loving Jesus and remaining in him. The Prayer of the Heart is in itself an inner act which no one else can see; therefore, we should invest in this great freedom by exercising this inner act abundantly. During the day, we have so many empty moments: for instance, when commuting, doing a manual job, housework. It is fruitful to take advantage of these moments in a spiritually effective way.

It is normal for the beginner in spiritual life to find it difficult to remember to practice this act during the day, because it is easier and requires no effort to allow work, duties, routine with all the inherent activity, worries and concerns which these entail to become all-engrossing. But when we start our day by practicing the Prayer of the Heart and *lectio divina*, the love of Jesus grows in us progressively, so remembering him and connecting with him becomes increasingly more spontaneous. Therefore, the beginner should not despair; on the contrary, he should "part the sea" of his time (like Moses) by being vigilant in practicing *lectio divina* daily and faithfully and by devoting the initial small amount of time allocated for the Prayer of the Heart.

Loving in Deeds or in Inner Acts?

In his first letter, St. John writes, "Little children, let us not love in word or speech but in deed and in truth" (1 John 3:18). Some think that practicing the Prayer of the Heart throughout the day does not have any value and that it would better if our love was "in deed and in truth" and that that should suffice. The answer to this is twofold:

1) The inner act is a real act which nourishes the core of our being, and we need to practice this vital act.

2) There is no contradiction between inner acts and deeds. We need to practice both. Furthermore, loving "in words" is also a real act which we should not underestimate: thus we do not tell the devil that we love him (St. Louis de Montfort).

In the second section of this third part, under the title "*Prayer of the Heart* and Ministry," we will see the relationship between the Prayer of the Heart, i.e., the inner act, and ministry/service, i.e., love in deeds, and it will become clearer to us how the inner act is at the root of our deeds.

Feeling or Not Feeling? How Can We Know and Discern?

God's action in the Prayer of the Heart happens essentially in our heart, which is an area which is beyond our consciousness, which cannot be reached by the senses of the body and the feelings of the soul. What we generally feel in our body and soul is a remote echo of God's work in our spirit. This feeling gradually establishes peace in the soul and quietness in the body. Sometimes God chooses to give the soul and/or the body: consolations, feelings and senses of his love, lights, knowledge, visions, healings, tears, spiritual delight, palpable peace, and so forth. These gifts are created and cannot be compared to the God's gift of himself to us in our heart where he gives us his divine and uncreated nature.

In the Prayer of the Heart, it is not mandatory for God to give us these consolations in the soul and/or the body. During the Prayer of the Heart, it is very possible (and is more usually the case) not to feel a great deal: the general "feeling"—the echo in the soul/body of what God is doing in the spirit—could be compared with the gentle trickling of water from a tap. Remember the *gentle breeze* that the Prophet Elijah felt when God made himself present to him (1 Kings 19:12–13) or the *manna* in the desert, which did not have a strong taste (Exodus 16:15). On the one hand, we should not expect to experience anything in the senses or in the feelings: these are created things and there is a danger we could come to idolize them. On the other hand, we do not go to Jesus for his *gifts* but for *himself*, naked on the cross.

Furthermore, when God leads us into deeper purification of the spirit, it is normal—and it is intentional on the part of God—to feel as if darkness were surrounding us. This does not mean that God is not working in us; on the contrary, it shows how close he is to us, and that he is realizing a deep purification (as all the filth of our being comes to the surface).

✝

How can we know if the connection with God during the Prayer of the Heart is working? How can we discern God's work in us during this silent moment? Considering the principles enunciated previously, we deduce that it is very dangerous and risky to evaluate the quality of our contact with God (whether it is happening or not) during the Prayer of the Heart on the basis of what we feel. In only very rare cases do some spiritual masters possess the gift of knowing the quality of our prayer. In normal cases, the spiritual director discerns God's work in the Prayer of the Heart by checking the following three points:

What Precedes the Prayer of the Heart

Listening to Jesus's word and putting it into practice (*lectio divina*) precedes the Prayer of the Heart, as Jesus states: "If a man loves me, he will keep my word, and my Father will love him, and we will come to him and make our home with him" (John 14:23). We see the conditional relationship between keeping Jesus's word (*lectio divina*) and the coming of the Trinity into our heart (Prayer of the Heart). In fact, *lectio divina* underpins the Prayer of the Heart, since it allows Jesus to grow in us, whilst it generates and strengthens the virtues in us. It greatly intensifies God's work in the Prayer of the Heart, as if it were compelling Him to love us anew. Whomsoever is faithful to Jesus's words and obedient to him during the day, opens wide the door to God's love in the Prayer of the Heart. Thus, by checking the quality of the practice of *lectio divina* one can be at peace about God's desire to give himself in the Prayer of the Heart, knowing that it will work. Otherwise, without joining *lectio divina* to the Prayer of the Heart we will remain like "dwarves," as St Teresa of Avila says.

The Prayer of the Heart Itself

It is necessary to learn to practice the Prayer of the Heart correctly: this is the goal of this book. Jesus's disciples said to him: "teach us how to pray" (Luke 11:1) because we are not born knowing how to pray and we cannot settle for spontaneity only in this vital matter. Without taking away simplicity and spontaneity, we need to learn how to make the act of the Prayer of the Heart in order to perfect it so that we can have direct contact with God within us. Sadly the faithful often ignore the elements of the act of oblation and how to do it. This is painful to watch, because the loss is incalculable! It is important for the spiritual director to check that the person has really learned to practice the act of offering, and that there are no obstacles to hinder its practice.

What Follows the Prayer of the Heart

It is important to know that spiritual life does not end with us having prayed. There is another reality, of equal importance: prayer life extends into the ways in which one who practices the Prayer of the Heart spends his/her day. We cannot separate the different moments of prayer from how we live our daily lives. Otherwise we would become spiritually schizophrenic; prayer and daily practice should be in harmony. Prayer influences the rest of our day, and vice-versa: the way we spend our day will affect the way we pray. Therefore, it is important to be faithful to our prayer life during the day. It is not reasonable to treat Jesus's body (our neighbor) badly during the day and then dare to seek intimacy with Jesus-the-head in the Prayer of the Heart. This is also one of the elements of discernment in spiritual direction.

Thoughts and Distractions

As we mentioned previously in the Existential Example, the Prayer of the Heart does not happen in the *mind* but in the *heart*. In a simple way, we showed the difference between them by showing the difference between our head (the skull) and our chest. There is a physical distance between them and nobody can mistake one for the other. We often think that praying consists in the words we have to say to God, and we forget the priority of "connecting" our heart to God (this happens in the act of offering ourselves).

Sometimes, in order to express the offering of himself to God and his desire and thirst for him, man needs words to say silently to God. For example, "O God, I entrust myself totally into your hands," or "As a hart longs for flowing streams, so longs my soul for you, O God" (Psalm 42:1).

Distractions in the Prayer of the Heart arise from the presence in our mind of involuntary thoughts, feelings, memories, imaginations, temptations, and so forth. The causes of distractions are human weakness, memories (the consequence of the involuntary action of the brain), physical exhaustion, temptations that come from outside of us, something exterior influencing us through our senses, sins (because they enslave us through bad habits which drive us away from God), as well as many other things. Involuntary distractions do not stop the Prayer of the Heart, because they occur in the mind while the Prayer of the Heart takes place in the heart.

If involuntary distractions occur, we need to address them as follows:

a) We need to calmly accept our weakness: a peaceful reaction attracts the Lord's peace.

b) We should repeat the act of offering ourselves—as we explained previously—in order for God to introduce us again into the fire of his love.

c) We must learn to recollect our thoughts and senses in order to weaken their influence over us, by remote and close preparation for the Prayer of the Heart.

Remote preparation: to lead a healthy life, balanced, ordered; to have a holy life; to learn the virtues of silence, self-discipline, asceticism, and to practice *lectio divina* well, because it adjusts our thoughts, purifies them, weakens the influence on us of distractions, and boosts the Prayer of the Heart.

Immediate preparation: dimming the ambient light in order to diminish exterior influences on us and in order to strengthen attention on the inner world; feel invited by the grace of an icon to pray in front of it.

d) We need to acquire the following daily habit: never remove our gaze from the Lord Jesus who is always at our side or within us, discovering his great love for us, since he never averts his gaze from us.

e) We could read a short passage from the Gospel; it will help us recollect our thoughts and hold ourselves in Jesus's presence.

f) Holding our rosary in our hands, we should repeat a short prayer that contains Jesus's and/or Mary's name.

Obstacles to the Prayer of the Heart:
Worries and Attachments

The most common obstacles to the Prayer of the Heart are hesitation, worries, lack of trust in God, attachment to somebody, attachments to ourselves or to something, putting conditions on our act of offering. The act of offering (which is the core of the Prayer of the Heart) in itself is very simple, but it relies on our freedom and personal choice. Through it we present to the Lord our dearest possession: our heart. Our heart takes off like a small bird in the sky of God's heart. However, we know that for a little bird a thread is like a rope, which prevents it from flying. Hesitation prevents the bird from taking off. Worries totally prevent flight, since they keep the mind busy with a created object—as opposed to God who is the Creator—like a problem or an argument, diverting it from God. Lack of trust in God causes the bird to lose direction, and it forgets that its resting place is in God. Being attached to something or someone, even something very superficial, prevents us from propelling ourselves towards God. Insistent attachment in itself, and the lack of offering the object of our attachment to God are direct obstacles to taking off, and a total contradiction of the movement. Sometimes we put conditions on our act of offering ("I give you myself with the condition that you give me this or that"). This, in itself, is due to an attachment to something created, revealing a lack of total trust in God by not giving him supremacy in our heart. All this defiles our heart, preventing the purification necessary to see God.

The remedy is to offer the obstacle to God in order to cut the rope or thread that prevents our heart from flying. The human being alone is capable of offering the obstacle because his active attachment to a creature constitutes the obstacle; and God respects the human being's freedom and choice in the extreme. "Offering the obstacle" is a free act which is dependent on the choice made by the individual. Offering the obstacle is, in fact, an act of the will; therefore, it does not always necessarily free us from continuing to experience the obstacle (and obviously it does not remove the object of our attachment, because it is exterior to ourselves) but it renders our heart free, making it really capable of taking off. God appreciates this act of our will immensely because, through it, we place God at the pinnacle of everything in our life and most especially above the obstacle.

Dryness and Perseverance

What shall we do if we do not feel anything during the Prayer of the Heart?

First, we do not practice the Prayer of the Heart because we want to feel something in our soul (mind and will) or in our body (senses). Anything that falls in the soul or in the body is something created, not the Creator. In the Prayer of the Heart, we go to Christ the King for himself and through faith and vision, not for ourselves. The act of faith gives us God himself. The act of faith in itself is pure: it puts us in God's hands, scattering any support that is not God, making of God the catalyst necessary for us to reach his heart. We are like the little child who abandons himself wholeheartedly into the arms of his mother where he rests in total contentment. Whosoever practices the Prayer of the Heart seeking consolation or light, feeling or knowledge takes a dead end which does not lead to God, because the Creator has been traded for the creature.

Second, during the Prayer of the Heart, the heart is immersed in God and, contrary to its normal habit, the mind finds itself unemployed; therefore, the challenge is to find a solution for the mind. We should not pay too much attention to the mind, in the same way as we would not to a "crazy" person, because it is often like a windmill, which never stops moving—it is constantly uttering thoughts—and the emptiness that the heart united to God dictates to the mind is new to it and it does not know how to deal with it.

Third, we need to quiet the mind and stop using it actively so that it does not prevent the action of God's grace in the heart, and so, in different ways:

a) The routine repetition of a short prayer keeps the mind busy with its words (stopping it from its normal chattering work), and concentrates the work on the desire and longing of the heart and the will, since the short prayer asks for the grace of God and his mercy.

b) Holding our rosary, even though it is a simple and humble physical act, helps to calm the mind and the imagination and brings them to the place where we are: in the heart (preventing the mind from straying).

c) Mary's intervention (through the invocation of her name and asking for her intercession) makes her come and put her hand around our heart, protecting the encounter with the Lord Jesus that occurs in it, greatly reducing the influence of emptiness in the mind and the distractions that result from it.

d) It is possible to read a short text from the Gospel in order to recollect our mind and senses around Jesus's presence in front of us or in us.

e) Praying in front of an icon exposes our entire being to the light of one of Jesus's mysteries. The icon's image speaks to the heart and recollects the thoughts.

f) Imitating a little child calms the work of our mind to a great extent enabling us to descend much faster into the heart, adopting the heart's language in our encounter with Jesus.

Perseverance and patience in the practice of the Prayer of the Heart will generate new habits for the mind that will make it more used to quietness, so step by step, its perplexity in the face of its idleness will diminish. The acceptance of not feeling anything and seeking to please God with love and faith are acts higher and purer than any others. They excavate in us a new space for God where he alone dwells: a space that becomes the solid nucleus of our being and the center of gravity in our dealings with the exterior world in our daily affairs.

When the Body Prays

The human being is one being, composed of a body, a soul, and a spirit, and each of these parts is composed of other parts. There is no human life on earth without a body and without consciousness. The human being is not normally saved while sleeping or unconscious: he needs to act. The body participates in all human acts from the highest to the most humble ones. For these reasons, the body has its own role in prayer life and in the Prayer of the Heart as well.

Daily life influences the body positively and negatively. Stress, physical effort, and exhaustion lower the body's readiness for prayer. For some people, this constitutes a real obstacle for elevating the heart so that it can enter into contact with God. We say "some" because the bed-ridden can receive the gift of prayer, for example, through short sighs or rapid glances at Jesus. Pain is a two-edged sword: it can elevate the human being to God (the elevators being love and the cross) or it can grind him down leading to distress and spiritual suffocation.

Usually, in the daily practice of the Prayer of the Heart, some people find they need—especially after a long day of work—some physical exercise (stretching, for example, basic yoga) in order to relax the body so that it does not become an obstacle to prayer. These exercises are not prayer, but they are a preparation for prayer.

When we pray, we express with our body the predispositions of our heart and soul. Prostrating, kneeling, standing, and bowing are all body postures which help us pray expressing different things. They are not prayer, but they express prayer because of the unity of the body, soul, and spirit. They are not conditions for prayer, since the sick person on his bed does not perform them and yet still prays—thank God! It is also important for the position of the body not to generate excessive pain or extreme discomfort (for example, kneeling for a long time) because it can become an obstacle to prayer or inflate our ego thinking that treating our body in this way pleases God. On the other hand, whoever wants to pray while being in a "horizontal position," after a while will obviously fall asleep. This is not, however, an admonishment of the excellent and important habit of taking up the Prayer of the Heart in bed before sleeping because it modifies the quality of our sleeping and makes us wake up in the same way we fall asleep: in Jesus.

Breathing

The Eastern tradition transmitted the Prayer of the Heart to us and called it the Jesus Prayer, because it is based on the repetition of a short prayer which has Jesus's name in it: "Lord Jesus Christ, Son of God, have mercy on me, a sinner." It is necessary to repeat this short prayer consistent with our breathing: "Lord Jesus Christ, Son of God"—(breathing in)—"have mercy on me, a sinner"—(breathing out). The function of breathing, from being purely physiological, becomes a spiritual tool to reach a state where breathing is not divorced from the act of "loving in the Holy Spirit." Did not Jesus breathe on his disciples in order to give them the Holy Spirit? (John 20:22) The Church continues to use this habit in various rites: the bishop breathes over the Chrism oil in order to consecrate it (Latin Rite); the priest breathes on the baptized during his baptism (Coptic and Byzantine rites); the priest also breathes when he exorcises.

Sometimes we misunderstand the relationship between breathing and the Prayer of the Heart (or Jesus Prayer). Some think that with their breathing they can control their prayer. Prayer is a grace we ask for and which we cannot force; therefore, breathing follows the grace of God and tries to blend with it, but never imposes itself on it.

At other times, the excess of concentration when making the offering of ourselves, with an intense attention to God and making a huge effort in order not to disturb the sacred encounter, unconsciously pushes us to lower the rhythm of our breathing or even stop it. This is a deviation and an error; we should put an end to this habit and try to breath in a normal and balanced way (neither faster nor slower than normal).

Whoever practices the Jesus Prayer has to remember the radical priority of the act of offering oneself over the repetition in accordance with our breathing.

Deepening the Prayer of the Heart

Whoever practices the Prayer of the Heart and *lectio divina* powerfully bolsters the growth of his spiritual life and goes through a journey of real transformation in Jesus. Step by step, the *old man* diminishes and the *new man* grows and, with him, the capacity for receiving God's action in us. Instead of being like the bed of a small stream capable of holding only a trickle of water (the grace of God), he becomes a wide riverbed, then a seabed, and then an ocean-bed. The abundance and elevation of the graces we can receive are proportionate to the degree of purification and transformation in Jesus.

The spiritual masters identified various stages of spiritual growth and with them different states of the Prayer of the Heart. Broadly speaking, they determined the necessity of purifying the senses (body and senses), the soul (mind, will, imagination, emotions) and the spirit (the highest part of the mind and will). After having finished this purification, the human being is received into the state of the *spiritual* betrothal, which is followed by the state of the *spiritual marriage*, wherein the human being lives in fullness, in the words of St. Paul: "I do not live anymore, it is Christ who lives in me" (Galatians 2:20). With Jesus and through Jesus, the human being participates with a new efficacy in the work of salvation. After that, the human being goes through new stages until he reaches the fullness of love, known as "dying in Jesus."

St. Teresa of Avila categorized the different stages of the Prayer of the Heart that go along with the stages of spiritual growth. Amongst the most important we have are 1) Meditation (discursive); 2) Prayer of Recollection (going inwardly to get close to Jesus in our heart); 3) Supernatural Quiet (beginning of the action of the Holy Spirit); 4) Prayer of Quiet (the heart only is united with God); 5) Prayer of Union (the heart and the conscious part are united with God); 6) Ecstasy; 7) Spiritual Betrothal; 8) Spiritual Marriage.

As a consequence, it is normal for anyone who is fervent in his spiritual life to experience many changes in himself and in his experience of God. He should then refer to the *spiritual master* in order not only to understand what God is doing in him, but also to know what to do in order to grow to the following stage and not hinder his growth or remain satisfied with the point he has reached.

Reading and Studying the Spiritual Masters

Spiritual culture plays a very important role in our spiritual life. On the one hand, it protects our spiritual life from the negative influences which reach us from the surrounding world; on the other, it is a favorable environment which supports and drives us on to strive in our daily spiritual effort.

Between the human heart and the world in which one lives there is nothing to protect the heart and thoughts from the ways, habits, and principles of the world. These negative influences threaten spiritual life, and they can very easily crush it if the thoughts of the person are not impregnated with a spiritual culture. This latter comes mainly from reading the lives of the saints and from studying the teachings of the spiritual masters.

Knowing the principles of spiritual life, its "monuments" and its teachings gives us a culture that will allow, like the good soil, the growth of the seed of spiritual life. Often spiritual life requires bold radical decisions that carry a different spirit, way of thinking, and habits from the ones of the world, so people seem "crazy" or "strange" to others; they could feel that being faithful to God is isolating them in some way from the surrounding world. The presence of saints and the example of their lives are not only a consolation to us, but they also provide a real support which can reassure us that we are on the right path. This is why reading is an opportunity to get closer to the saints in order to get to know them, so that they become our new friends who give us necessary support in our arduous journey.

No doubt, the spiritual master and the spiritual friends who live this spiritual life also play a similar role to the saints and to spiritual teaching. We should constantly strive to avail ourselves on this spiritual journey of these rich and necessary aids that God gives us in the Church.

"Spiritual culture" does not mean just accumulating information; it is also comprised of elements of our life which support and elevate spiritual life. Spiritual culture is a living human environment which receives and embraces spiritual life. Amongst its elements, we have science, art, media, social media, and entertainment. All this can be colored in a way that is in harmony with spiritual life or in contradiction with it. This depends on us and on our choices. Therefore, we need constantly to be making an effort to create and grow elements of spiritual culture in order not to have an unprotected spiritual life.

There is a difference between reading and studying. Studying—analyzing, ordering and discerning—incites us to spend more time learning and benefiting from its lights, and thanks to this effort the text we are reading becomes a channel for the grace of God. Studying spiritual life is the source of many refined graces. Whoever stops with humility and reverence in front of the treasures that Jesus deposited for us in the books of the spiritual masters disposes himself to receive these graces.

Since the Prayer of the Heart is still—very sadly—little known, there is a greater need to work hard in order to build a strong personal and community culture in this field in order to support its practice and to secure it spreading. The important books on the Prayer of the Heart are, among those from the East: *The Way of a Pilgrim*, *The Philokalia*, Evagrius Ponticus, "On Prayer," the teachings of the Hesychast Fathers, Diadochus of Photicea, St. Maximus

the Confessor, St. Symeon the New Theologian, St. Gregory Pala-
mas, and St. Silouan the Athonite. Among those from the West are
the works of St. Teresa of Avila (*Autobiography, Way of Perfection,
The Interior Castle*), St. John of the Cross, St. Thérèse of Lisieux,
Blessed Elisabeth of the Trinity, and St. Louis de Montfort (*True
Devotion to Our Lady*).

PRAYER OF THE HEART
AND THE LIFE OF THE CHURCH

✝

The Prayer of the Heart and Baptism

Baptism is the gate to all the sacraments, and it introduces us as well
to life with Jesus since it removes the obstacles between us and
Jesus; more than this, it immerses us in the Father, in the Son, and
in the Holy Spirit. Baptism in Greek means "immersion." When we
are baptized, we are immersed in and out of the water and three
times (as in the Eastern rites, which have kept the rite of immersion), but in reality having been immersed, we should remain as
such, *immersed* in the Holy Trinity, and never emerge. The role and
responsibility of the individual—of course with the help of the
grace of God—is to maintain this immersion, keeping in constant
contact with God, since communication with God is vital (the para-
ble of the vine and the branches in John 15:1-11). The function of the
Prayer of the Heart is to help us remain *in Christ* and to be in communication with him. This is why St. John emphatically stresses the
necessity for us to remain in Jesus: "dwell in me" (John 15:4).

✝

Baptism also allows us to participate in Jesus's priesthood. With
Jesus and in him, it becomes possible for each of the faithful to offer
himself as a sacrifice acceptable to God (see 1 Peter 2:5). The priestly
function requires a priest, a sacrifice, God, an altar, and a fire. When
the faithful person participates in Jesus's priesthood, he becomes, in
Jesus, a priest and a sacrifice (an offering). In order for priestly wor-

ship to happen, the faithful should offer the sacrifice (himself) on the altar (Jesus, the "cornerstone" and the "fulcrum"), through the fire (the Holy Spirit, the elevating and transforming power) to God the Father. This authority which Jesus gives to the faithful is indeed a wondrous mystery, a deposit entrusted to the hands of the baptized, in which they should invest daily.

The Prayer of the Heart is the framework of the practice of the faithful priesthood, since in it we elevate our heart (which represents our whole being) to God as a real sacrifice, in spiritual worship (Romans 12:1).

The Prayer of the Heart and the Eucharist

The Eucharist, or the Mass, has two parts, as the Gospel (Jesus's public life) has two parts. The first part is Jesus's teaching, and this gives us the Table of the Word of God in the Mass. The second part is Jesus's passion, death and resurrection and this gives us the Table of Jesus's Body and Blood. At the first table, we eat Jesus's words which are "spirit and life" (John 6:63), while at the second table we receive the Body and Blood of Jesus. Both are a very substantial meal (they are in fact one Table, one Lord), and we do not often have the opportunity to digest, assimilate, and benefit from them. This is why it is important to give enough time to activate that "food." This opportunity is given to us when we practice *lectio divina* and the Prayer of the Heart. The first is the extension of the Table of the Word and it helps us listen to Jesus's word and put it into practice; the second, the Prayer of the Heart, is the extension of the Table of the Body and Blood of Jesus, and more specifically the prolongation of the very moment of Communion.

Receiving Communion is in itself a wondrous moment of *manducation* (action of chewing food), but in real life it lasts only a very short moment, usually just a few minutes. Jesus finds himself not being able to give us an entire meal, since, once the Mass is ended, we engage with the noise of chatter or of the street. In fact, through negligence, we allow the effect of Communion in us to vanish or to be diluted without communicating all its power, both purifying and transforming.

Truly, Jesus whom we receive will never be lost, since "the gifts and the call of God are irrevocable" (Romans 11:29). But the effect of Communion on us depends on us, as to whether we are under his influence or not. The Communion received is a sacred deposit and a treasure entrusted to us in our heart, but how often do we abandon him in exchange for the exterior world, forgetting the benefits of the Rays of his Love on us? Therefore, we must not leave him alone in our heart: we need to learn to come back constantly to that treasure and expose ourselves, at length, to the beams of the sun of his love. This is precisely the function of the Prayer of the Heart. It helps us to return to Jesus dwelling in our heart, and exercises us to remain the longest possible time with him, since he is our temple. As we can see, the relationship between the Prayer of the Heart and Communion is deep and direct.

The Prayer of the Heart and Lectio Divina

It is possible to say that the relationship between *lectio divina* and the Prayer of the Heart is of the same type of relationship as between the Liturgy of the Word and the Liturgy of the Body and Blood of Jesus in the Mass. It is the same relationship that exists between the two parts of the Gospel. In the first part, Jesus words nourish the conscious part of our being (mind and will); in the second, Jesus's Passion, Death, and Resurrection nourish the whole being, especially the deep supra-conscious roots (the heart or spirit).

The tree provides a good metaphor. The visible part of the tree (trunk, branches, and leaves) needs light and air; this symbolizes the conscious part of the human being, its food is *lectio divina*. The invisible part of the tree (the roots) needs water and minerals; it represents the supra-conscious part of us for which the food is the Prayer of the Heart. The tree is one, the human being is one; Jesus our bread is one, and the Table of the Mass is one.

The specific food of the *lectio divina* strengthens the structure of the human being, and boosts—in a new way—the efficacy of the Prayer of the Heart. The Prayer of the Heart's food gives depth and foundation to the human being and to the practice of *lectio divina*.

The sap goes from the roots to the leaves, silently but efficiently. The energy of the sunrays is transformed into a chemical and biological energy which nourishes the entire tree. We cannot separate the practice of the Prayer of the Heart from the practice of *lectio divina* (each one at its proper time): they are the two legs that help us progress in spiritual life.

The Prayer of the Heart and Knowing God

Jesus says, "Eternal life is that they know you the only true God" (John 17:3). Eternal life is God's life in us. From the first moment the grace of God starts to work in us, eternal life begins as well. This is why *knowing God* is a central issue and an absolute necessity in our life here on earth. It reminds us of the First Commandment saying that we must "love God" and that we must give supremacy to his love. Whoever loves God knows him and whoever knows God loves him.

The Prayer of the Heart plays a crucial role in the knowledge of God. It offers God the space to show us himself and to pour his love into us. It is an encounter—a love encounter—with Jesus the Bridegroom. Our choice to daily and faithfully dedicate a sacred time to meet him is a great sign of love in his eyes; it does not make him hesitate to give us love in return for our love. Whosoever perseveres in this daily meeting transforms his relationship with God into an authentically deep friendship, making him enter day after day deeper into new depths within God. The life of the human being then becomes a chain of revelations or discoveries about God himself and the "bowels of his mercy" (Luke 1:78) which surpasses our mind and imagination. Whosoever gives his life to God with generosity will experience God's royal munificence.

Without doubt, whoever studies theology and practices the Prayer of the Heart daily understands and tastes from within the elements of dogma and reaches their core with greater ease—with the help of the Holy Spirit. Whoever addresses theological topics with his mind helped by the general light of faith resembles a traveler walking on his feet, while whoever adds to it the Prayer of the Heart, will be introduced to the intimacy of God: he will resemble one who flies to his destination. We cannot separate the Prayer of the Heart from the study of theology; the ancient spiritual masters used to call "theology" the highest spiritual experience and growth, because the human being would have reached union with Jesus, dwelling then in the Trinity: in the Son, before the Father, through the Holy Spirit. "Theology" alludes here to the "knowledge of the very nature of God" because the knowledge one has here is a direct revelation of the Father.

The Prayer of the Heart: Oneself, Neighbor, and the Church

First, the Prayer of the Heart is an intimate encounter with God where he pours his Holy Spirit into us. The primary action of the Holy Spirit in us is to purify us: he eliminates from our heart all that is not God. This operation is progressive, and normally happens from the direction of our outer being (the senses) to the inside (the spirit). God is light and the more he penetrates new layers of depth in us, the more his light shines in them and offers us new knowledge and understanding about ourselves that no human being can know or guess with his own capacity. Not even the best psychoanalyst or philosopher—however intimate—can get as close compared to the knowledge of oneself that God offers.

There is an immense difference between the theoretical knowledge we get from reading and studying (philosophy, psychology, psychoanalysis, theology) and the spiritual knowledge resulting from the action of the Holy Spirit in us. Experiencing the fire of God is different from conversing about it from a distance. The Prayer of the Heart enkindles the fire of that encounter and leads us, step by step, to a new knowledge and to a humility that is impossible to fake because it is the result of the experience of the weight of the "Arm of the Lord" (Isaiah 53:1) and of his holiness. Whoever studies theology is unable to forget this.

Knowing God and knowing oneself are two sides of the same coin; and they grow directly proportional to each other. Step by step, the grace of God uncovers to the human being his nothingness while at the same time revealing God's mercy. If the human being were not supported by the growing knowledge of God's mercy on him, he would not be able to bear the vision of his nothingness unveiled to him by the Holy Spirit during prayer.

✝

Second, there is a profound and direct relationship between *knowing oneself* and *knowing one's neighbor*. Whoever knows himself in the Holy Spirit receives a new humility which makes him closer to others and more understanding, thus discovering Jesus in others, being non-judgmental but merciful to them and serving them. Really knowing oneself under God's light is the best way and the best grace, since it progressively unites man with his fellow humans. With this deep vision, any animosity toward any person is gradually dissipated. In this journey one discovers that people whom one once considered to be enemies are, at the end of the day, poor miserable humans—not more and not less than he—deserving of divine mercy. He feels that he and his brother are in the same situation, and continues to ask for mercy for himself and for his brother.

God gives his Holy Spirit in the Prayer of the Heart, which makes it the fundamental and practical source of knowledge of one's neighbor—understanding him from the inside and not from the outside. The more people practice this prayer, the more society will change and people will be united and merciful to each other.

The practice of the Prayer of the Heart introduces us into new depths in the Mystery of the Church: Jesus's Mystical Body. Jesus reveals to us that the Church does not only consist of the visible members that we see and their deeds, but consists of far more.

Undoubtedly, all this is of great importance to anyone who studies theology. Experience and fruitful knowledge of theology is of greater input than mere intellectual knowledge. There is a constant pendulum movement in whoever studies theology: from taste to understanding, and from understanding to taste; the first movement fosters the second and vice-versa.

Offering Our Emotions

When we love God and our neighbor, we use common expressions like: "heart," "emotions," and so forth. In reality, in order to love we use a main faculty of the soul: the will. If you want to love, this means that you loved.

Without knowing it, we dedicate the upper part of our heart and of our emotions to our relationship with God and to our piety in general. In loving our neighbor and more especially the strong emotional love involved in loving a father, mother, child, partner, or friend, we dedicate to that love the lower, warmer part of our heart. This part of our heart makes us feel the warmth of love and its fervor. For instance, when we fall in love, the part of our heart which is involved is the lower human and emotional part. Obviously, this part is not used in our relationship with God, in our love for him and our piety in general. We do not make this distinction on purpose or with awareness. It does not naturally occur to us to give to God with the warmer part of our heart or to be involved with Him in the same way.

✝

What does God want from our emotions? This question addresses an issue that will appear for many as new or strange. In reality, through their life and witness, the saints help us a great deal to understand how we need to love Jesus. Their love and passion for Jesus open up new horizons to us which we could not imagine in our wildest Christian dreams. We are astonished to see a saint loving Jesus the Bridegroom with a passion that resembles the passionate love a wife has for her husband; this inflames our heart to a new love. This raises our attention to an important point in the First Commandment. There, God says that we need to love him with "all" our heart and "all" our energy. He did not say "part."

Jesus goes further and orientates our emotional-heart in a new and powerful direction when he says, "He who loves father or mother more than me is not worthy of me; and he who loves son or daughter more than me is not worthy of me" (Matthew 10:37). This means that we need to put our emotions for Jesus higher than any other emotion, in a way that they become the foundation and the principle of any other emotion. This is indeed a sacrifice of Abrahamic proportions (Abraham offered to God the one he loved most: his son). We deduce from this that if we want to love Jesus God and Bridegroom, we need to put into his hands, or better into his heart, our emotions, and our loved ones, together with our capacity to be passionately and humanly in love. He is indeed the true Bridegroom who loves us with all his being and who gave himself to us totally, and no human husband can do that. Being perfect God and perfect human, he alone can totally quench our deepest thirst to love and be loved even at a human level.

In order for our heart to be inflamed in a greater way in the Prayer of the Heart (and this point is of the utmost importance), in order to discover Jesus the Bridegroom's passionate love for us, we need to put all our emotions and desires into the furnace of his heart. The saints proved very clearly that when Jesus the Bridegroom loves us and inflames our heart with the fire of his love, there is no other love or passion on earth that can equal it. Let us not be greedy with Jesus. Let us give him all our human emotions—we will never regret it. He is royal in his richness and generosity when he loves our human heart—better than any human passion, more fulfilling both in human and spiritual terms.

The Prayer of the Heart and Ministry

Jesus chose to share his mission with us. For this purpose he called 12 apostles and 72 disciples, and many others. He taught them, formed them, and sent them out in his name. After his death, resurrection, and ascension, and the coming of the Holy Spirit, they all started their mission in a new way. All these steps in their preparation teach us the spiritual stages where those called by Jesus are purified and mature in order for the Holy Spirit to be able to guide them to a greater level of freedom, making their mission divine and not merely the product of human endeavor. Jesus warned us repeatedly not to pitch ourselves in his service without his order and guidance, saying to the ones who think that they can prophesy, cast out devils, and make miracles in his name: "I never knew you; depart from me, you evildoers" (Matthew 7:23).

The Prayer of the Heart exposes us to the light of the Holy Spirit and to its work in us. The roots of the human being cannot be purified without his work. Purity allows God to possess our being, guiding us in our deeds and our service (ministry) from inside. With this purifying operation the Kingdom of God in us becomes bigger and under the action of the Holy Spirit our heart changes from a "heart of stone" to a "heart of flesh" (see Ezekiel 36). This is why St. John of the Cross strongly invites those who minister and preach to practice the Prayer of the Heart at great length—doubling the hours one spends serving—in order for the work not to be of little or of no value, or even damaging in effect.

We see then how the deep work of God in the Prayer of the Heart is not only fundamental to spiritual life, but that it is the source and the starting point of service and ministry. The servant is a witness to Jesus, and his purity of heart allows him to see Jesus (Matthew 5:8); the Prayer of the Heart is the crucible where our heart is placed and purified by the Holy Spirit. The Prayer of the Heart offers a new (and always renewable) experience of God's love for us; if the servant does not experience it, what will he give to his brother during his ministry? Hollow hands have nothing to offer!

Ministry is the service of a brother in Christ, either baptized or called to be (as indeed we are all called). As a result, we present true worship to Jesus. When Jesus calls us to serve him, he entrusts part of his sacred body to our care. In order to enter into the state of service and this vision of things, we need first to meet Jesus the head, through the Prayer of the Heart. In prayer and through it, Jesus presents to us members of his body, inviting us to receive them into our hearts, in a sublime spiritual hospitality. We cannot serve a human being in Christ without these conditions. This is why Jesus laid great importance on praying for our brothers and for our enemies. "Enemy" here does not always mean "a person far from Jesus," but it always means "a person far from me," a person I have not yet received in my heart. With the aid of the Holy Spirit alone and through God's mercy which we experience during the Prayer of the Heart, we become capable of receiving our brother. In this way, we are able to live in a new and deep way the Holy Spirit's Commandment: "Do not neglect to show hospitality to strangers, for thereby some have entertained angels unawares. Remember those who are in prison, as though in prison with them; and those who are ill-treated, since you also are in the body" (Hebrews 13:2–3).

From this we understand that the Prayer of the Heart is not only the starting point of service and ministry, but it is the spiritual crucible or furnace in which ministry takes place.

✝

As we said above, when Jesus sends us to serve, he entrusts our brother to our care. For this reason we carry our brothers in prayer. This responsibility is a deep aspect of the faithful priesthood. Without knowing it, we carry our brother in us and the Holy Spirit ties us together—he is the bond of love—so our prayer is for ourselves and for our brother; our brother's feelings become ours as well, and the work of the Holy Spirit happening in us is extended spontaneously to him.

It is normal for any pain or annoyance which occurs during the day (regardless of whether we know the reasons) is carried forward in us when we start the Prayer of the Heart. Exposing ourselves during prayer to the ray of the Holy Spirit allows God to clarify and work out what has happened in us, because we are, with our brother, one in Christ; and the fruits of salvation work in both of us together. In this way service also occurs, and everything is elevated in Christ and in the Holy Spirit to God the Father, an image of what happens during the Mass. This offering is accompanied by gratitude, thanksgiving, and praise to Jesus who is "all and in all" (Colossians 3:11).

In this way, the Holy Spirit accomplishes the mission, seals, and crowns it. Let us not forget that the Prayer of the Heart, while being an operation of being born again, happens not only in the presence of Our Lady, but within her, where only God-Fire operates.

The Prayer of the Heart
and Non-Christian Meditation

Each religion has its own mystical or contemplative ways through which the human being tries to enter in direct contact with God. Each method of meditation in the non-Christian religions and in the more modern ways of meditation has its own foundations, conditions, and techniques. We can neither negate nor ignore the extensive and rich analysis that characterizes many of them. But, at the same time, we cannot ignore what is specific and unique to Christianity. We cannot ignore the richness of the Christian Spiritual Tradition and the treasures of the teachings of both the Eastern and Western spiritual masters and schools.

The speed and ease of today's means of communication and travel bring closer to us—in the West—other teachings around meditation. More traditional Christian and Christian-centered societies today are not only surrounded by Far Eastern spiritualities, but they are no longer the center of society. The challenges are serious since we sit as equals. Yoga, with all its levels (Transcendental Meditation, Zen Buddhism, Sufi Dhikr), and other spiritual practices of the East are commonly taught and practiced everywhere today.

It is important for our evaluation, knowledge and experience—both at a personal and community level—to be on a par with a wisdom and maturity which does honor to Christ. If a substantial part of non-Christian techniques of meditation has a very high level of analysis, this should not eclipse two necessities:

1) The necessity to study, know, and experience the power of the Holy Spirit and the efficiency of His Work, swift and direct, and the efficiency of the experience of the Risen Lord, present amongst us and in us.

2) The necessity to learn, know, and experience the teachings of the Christian spiritual masters and schools. Their richness—spread over 2000 years—is sadly very little known.

This devastating ignorance makes it easy for us to pray at two extremes of the spectrum:

1) For the Christian, the first extreme is to negate and exclude caustically and fanatically without discernment anything that is not Christian, saying that it comes from the Devil. The correct discernment requires from us to keep anything that is good that falls into our hands, because anything good belongs to Jesus even if it is a "smoldering wick" (Matthew 12:20).

2) For the Christian, the other extreme is to accept, with a strange, casual blindness, some techniques of meditation available in the market and even to become a zealous promoter of them, ignoring the work of the grace of God and its power and all that Jesus brought us in power, glory, efficiency, and healing.

Conclusion

The Necessity to Practice on a Daily Basis: A Christian Question

In this book we have addressed the key questions of the Prayer of the Heart and examined its place in our Christian life. It is, as St. John of the Cross states, "the source of all good," and it is not possible to have such a treasure within reach and not use it. The importance of the Prayer of the Heart is of vital and radical importance. Without it, our spiritual life becomes impoverished and after a while its riverbed dries up. Without God's love which he pours into our blood during the Prayer of the Heart, our deeds, services, and projects become a "resounding brass, or a clanging cymbal" (1 Corinthians 13:1). "The smallest act of pure love is more profitable to the Church, than all other good works together" (St. John of the Cross, *Spiritual Canticle*). The Prayer of the Heart is the backbone of the Church, keeping it incorruptible, connected to God, uniting heaven and earth, having placed her heart in the hands of God. Without it we do not receive Love from God, and the result is that "apostles would not preach the Gospel and martyrs would not shed their blood" (St. Thérèse of the Child Jesus).

Our daily reality makes us live in a dense, uninterrupted whirl which holds us in thrall. Our weakness does not allow us to prevail upon that huge obstacle. We should not despair, though: whoever asks will receive. In order to overcome and break the limitations of this flow and to create a new space for God during the day, we need to start with easy steps. Let us make this prayer then:

Jesus,
you made me understand the vital importance
of the Prayer of the Heart in my life,
I offer myself and all my life to you,
asking you, with humility and great determination,
to graciously show me how and when
to start being faithful to you,
with 10 minutes in the morning and 10 in the evening.

O Lord Jesus, give me the strength and perseverance
never to despair of my weakness,
and to be faithful to this daily encounter with You.

✝

We put this prayer into the hands of Our Lady, relying on her all-powerful intercession. Our Lady is the necessary sacred space who allows us to live the Prayer of the Heart daily, because she embraced Jesus and kept him in her heart, he whom heavens cannot contain (see 1 King 8:27). The Blessed Mother's heart is the one which prays, since her heart is the chapel of the Prayer of the Heart. As her children, our duty is to respond to her invitation in our heart in order for her to pray in us and with us and us with her. As the New Moses, Mary opens a way for us through the waters of daily events, leading us, leading us to victory, in such a way that we may never dissipate any grace that God wishes to give us.

The Necessity of Making the
Prayer of the Heart More Widespread

The prayer of the Christian faithful to our heavenly Father is characterized by simplicity and familiarity, but there is a difference between this and spontaneity. Man is meant to grow and learn everything, even prayer, which is why Jesus's disciples said to him: "Lord, teach us to pray, as John taught his disciples" (Luke 11:1). The Church's life is full of spiritual masters whom Jesus sent like the prophets (see Matthew 23:34), giving them the graces necessary to teach us about prayer and spiritual life in general and the Prayer of the Heart in particular. Our duty and responsibility is to strive to learn how to pray from them, especially since prayer has great depths and therefore there are many things to learn which are of vital importance. Prayer for the Christian is *not optional*, on the contrary it is a vital duty of inestimable value, which is why the Word of God invites us to "pray incessantly" (1 Thessalonians 5:17). We need to seek with effort and perseverance to learn the Prayer of the Heart, because it is the only prayer which will allow us to attain to the state of incessant prayer, the state of union with Jesus. Doctrine on prayer is available to us and books are readily available; both are talents offered to us, and we will have to give account for these one day.

God is everything in the life of man. He opened his heart and his being to us when he sent his Son to us, unveiling his intimate being, expressing to us his thirst and love for us. He deserves our whole and undivided attention; it is not fair to give him only the crumbs of our time and energy. He is our hope, our portion, and inheritance. For if we do not give him all the importance he deserves, we will receive him neither in this life nor in the next. The goal of our life on earth is to discover God and to plunge into his depths to obtain him totally and to be transformed in him. If we do not seize the opportunity in order to discover this treasure, we will miss it for all eternity. Christian life is much more than a choice between paradise and hell, between salvation and eternal damnation. It is an open gate allowing us to discover God's Being, to sail in his beauty and dissolve in it. This gate is the Prayer of the Heart and the ship which allows us to sail in him is the Prayer of the Heart. May God give us the humility and sensitivity to understand his heart and respect his numerous initiatives, which are knocking at the door of our heart and giving us the opportunity to respond generously to him and to discover how royally he bestows his graces.

✝

The teachings of the Prayer of the Heart are the richest treasure in the Church; therefore, we need to keep them alive through lucid translations, critical publications, and explanations which help the modern reader to understand them. Spiritual masters for our times should be prepared through untiring efforts, daily practice, and discernment undertaken in full humility and wisdom. The Church authorities should ensure the preparation of new masters and make available institutes and special schools to teach and transmit spiritual life in broad terms and the Prayer of the Heart in particular.

Whoever starts his journey trained in the Prayer of the Heart and begins to practice what he has learned, and whoever has found a master who can guide him, may feel a spontaneous urge to transmit what he has received. If he perseveres and if he is chosen, he should receive a higher formation which will help him, in his turn, to transmit to others, with precision and faithfulness, what he has received. This is why, in this context, the Church encourages lay people to play their part in this responsibility: "The Holy Spirit gives to certain of the faithful the gifts of wisdom, faith and discernment for the sake of this common good which is prayer (spiritual direction). Men and women so endowed are true servants of the living tradition of prayer" (*Catechism* 2690).

Appendix: On Icons

As we mention icons in the second part of this book, we need to better understand the theology and spirituality behind them and their impact on our practice of the Prayer of the Heart.

The Icon

An icon is a "painting" depicting one of Jesus's mysteries, which follows canonical rules in order to express, along theological lines and colors, the contour of a mystery, allowing the person in front of it to enter this mystery and to receive its grace. The icon is an aesthetic representation of theology: the extension of the presence of Jesus and of his mysteries among us, expressed in a theological way, which helps us worship through our senses.

The invisible and non-palpable God became visible and palpable in the Son Incarnate (see 1 John 1:1–2), and worshiping him is right and just, since he is "God among us." When we see Jesus, palpable in his humanity, we do not stop at his human nature; on the contrary, we plunge into the depths of his divinity in order to receive his divine life (see John 20:30–31). The acts of faith and contemplation take us from the palpable and the bodily in Jesus to his divine nature (see John 20:27–28).

The icon is a special grace among the graces of the Incarnation, and is an extension of it, since its theological language allows Jesus and the mysteries of his life to be present among us and to be available to worship. The icon is very closely bound to Jesus and to the Incarnation and to its consequences in our life after the Ascension of Jesus and the coming of the Holy Spirit.

The Conditions for Worship

In the Old Testament God warned man not to make any images of him or of any other being (remember the Golden Calf), so that the image would not become, in the heart of man, a god he worshipped: "I am the LORD your God, who brought you out of the land of Egypt, out of the house of bondage. You shall have no other gods before me. You shall not make for yourself a graven image, or any likeness of anything that is in heaven above, or that is in the earth beneath, or that is in the water under the earth; you shall not bow down to them or serve them; for I the LORD your God am a jealous God" (Exodus 20:2–5). This warning is part of God's pedagogy and education which he gave to man in order to prepare him for salvation in his only begotten Son. God taught the human being that his very nature is not created and, therefore, it is not possible to exchange it with anything created. This is why worship goes only to God.

The heart of the worshiper should not confuse the divine, uncreated, invisible nature with created nature, because worship should be addressed only to God. "Not confusing" does not mean separating the Creator from the creature, since the latter speaks about the former (see Romans 1:19–20). The distinction here between the Creator and the creature is neither a separation nor a fusion. We should add that the holy scriptures say that God created the heart of the worshipper "in his image and likeness." This means that God put something inexpressible in man's make-up: an amazing capacity to communicate and to enter into direct intimacy with him. In doing so, God put a limit on the infinite distance which exists between the Creator and the creature.

With the Incarnation, God came closer to the man in a way that surpasses our understanding, and He did so out of love. The two natures, divine and human, have been united in one Person, the Person of the Eternal Son. In addition, with the Incarnation, the Eternal Son unites himself with every human being in order to save him. As we know, in the one Christ, the Eternal Son Incarnate, there is no fusion or confusion of the two natures; they are united, without separation. The invisible God became visible, the inaudible became audible, the non-palpable became palpable (see 1 John 1:1–4). Because of the unity of Jesus's Person he is legitimately called God. When people touched Jesus, they touched God. When people prostrated themselves in front of Jesus, they did so in front of God. When we receive the Body of Jesus in the Mass, we truly receive God.

The consequence of the Incarnation is that the inaudible Eternal Word gave us words that we can hear and transmit. These words are "spirit and life" (John 6:63); we do not have the right to change these words because they express in ways comprehensible to the human mind the divinity of God and his mysteries.

We may deduce from this that it is possible to have "created words" which the human mind can understand but at the same time which, just like one of the mysteries of Jesus, are capable of transmitting divine life to us. As we have said, man cannot modify or change these words and their theological meaning. Their understanding and their transmission follow theological laws. It is our duty to transmit these words faithfully, according to the rules of faith, as Jesus commanded us to do. We need to evangelize.

Since the Incarnation made the invisible God visible, we have acquired the right to paint a picture of the visible God. When we see a picture or an icon of Jesus, which we venerate with devotion, or worship before it, we do not bow to a piece of paper or to wood, but to the one who is represented on them. The icon is richer than any piece of plastic art. The icon is essentially a theological language and not just a work of aesthetic expression. The latter falls under the category of "Art," while the icon—even if it uses the plastic mode of expression—falls under the category of "Theology." The icon offers us its own guidelines: lines, symbols, colors. The writer (and not the painter) of the icon uses these tools in order to express theologically one of God's mysteries. One needs to follow the rules of general theology and of the theology of icons. In this way, the lines, symbols, and colors become theological expressions.

The icon proceeds from two things: from this gift that Jesus gave the Church—the writing of icons—and from the spiritual and theological life of the writer of the icon. The iconographer has to be very well trained in spiritual life and in the practice of contemplation, in theology, and in the science of writing icons. This is why often (but not always) the writer of the icon is a monk. Before writing the icon he needs to prepare himself at length by fasting, praying, and contemplating in order for God to give him the grace of contemplating the mystery he is about to write on the wood. This is why the Church sets special prayers to consecrate the call of this person for this sacred mission and prayers and a special blessing for the icon when it is offered to the faithful for worship.

God wants us to enter into his mysteries through the inspired writer, and this is what differentiates the painted image from the written icon endowed as it is with exceptional inspiration from the Lord. As it becomes possible for us to see heavenly things as they are, and not as we imagine them to be in our mind (idols), the icons make us see the truth from the angle of vision bestowed upon the writer by God. This helps us see the considerable difference between, on the one hand, the painted image, fruit of the imagination, influenced by the emotions of the painter and his artistic background, and, on the other, the real contemplation and the ineffable inspiration through which God wants to unveil to us something new about one of the mysteries of heaven; this is what gives the icon venerability and respect.

The Place of the Icon in Prayer Life

Prayer is direct communication between God and us. The condition for this contact to happen is for it to be done "in spirit and in truth." "Spirit" here means Holy Spirit and "truth" here means Jesus. We need to be "in Jesus" in order for this direct communication with God to happen. The icon brings us close to Jesus, since it reminds us first of all of his human nature. The Holy Spirit elevates our heart from Jesus's human nature to his divinity. We understand then the centrality of the role of the icon in our prayer life.

We are not angels; therefore, when God wanted to speak and communicate with us he became man. When we want to listen to him and to speak to him we need to follow the same logic, the logic of the Incarnation, the logic which takes into account our human nature, as both rational and sensible beings. It is a sign of humility and of great orthodoxy to have recourse to icons in order to reach God and to communicate with him.

The Elements of the Icon

The theological purpose of the icon gives the latter its meaning and its spiritual efficacy, as well as shaping its aesthetic expression. This is why all the elements of the icon converge to serve the theological purpose. Therefore the aesthetic expression cannot be disjointed or separated from the theological contents and its limits.

The first element of the icon is the spiritual architecture of the drawing; the lines used express the mystery which we contemplate. The second element is color, where each one is suffused with theological meaning (gold, for example, alludes to the divine nature). Shapes and other means of expression used in the formulation of the icon respect specific rules transmitted faithfully in order to avoid departing from the framework of accepted theological expression. This is why icons often avoid using detail and decorative elements which do not convey any specific meaning.

The Most Widespread Icon

The most widespread icon is that of Our Lady and the Child Jesus. It is striking to observe that there are many icons which express mysteries which are more important than this one, like the Trinity and the Crucifixion. Furthermore, we know that the first icon the iconographer has to start with, is the icon of the Transfiguration, even though the most widespread icon is a different one: the icon of Mary and the Child Jesus which is altogether simpler and closer to our weak human nature. This icon is a direct reflection of the mystery of Christian worship at work in us.

In this icon, Jesus is the Eternal Son Incarnate, perfect man and perfect God. He is all that we need, and our worship is directed to him because he is God (often this icon depicts Jesus's clothes in gold, alluding to his divinity). On this icon we find in Mary the embodiment of perfect worship directed to Christ the Incarnate God: this perfection is expressed by the fact that Mary embraces and contains Jesus and that he does the same to her (see the movement of his arms). God offers us a place in this perfect worship in spirit and truth embodied by Mary: this can be seen in the gaze Our Lady directs towards us and in the movement of her hand, disclosing the way to Jesus. From her eyes to her hand, through her heart, Mary introduces us in her and through her, to the same intimacy and union she has with Jesus, so that we may have life. What we see in the icon is in fact what happens in our depths as is shown in the following diagram.

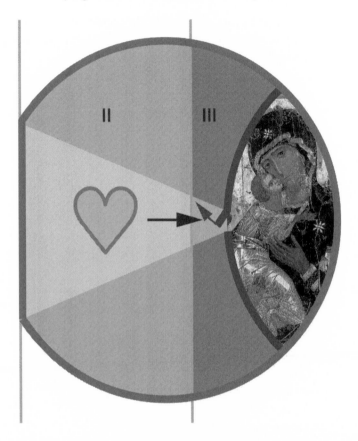

This icon introduces us into the circulation of love existing between Jesus and Mary: our place is in Mary. It is the best embodiment of the Prayer of the Heart.

What Happens When We
Pray before the Icon of the Mother of God

The writer of an icon cannot write it if he is not himself, pre-eminently, living the mystery he is writing. Jesus gives him the grace to contemplate one of his mysteries and introduces him into it. Jesus confers on those who pray in front of the icon a share in this contemplation and in this introduction in Him. The icon is an open window on God and on one of his mysteries, and it is open to us and ready to draw us into itself. After the consecration of the icon and the blessing, when the faithful stands before it, the grace of the icon draws him into this mystery.

Through Mary's eyes and her gaze upon us, and by her pointing the way to Jesus, we can enter into the mystery expressed in the icon: Mary, Mother of Mercy and our mother, embraces us in her, giving us her eyes and her heart in order to worship Jesus our God in truth. Through and with Mary we are able to contemplate Jesus and to love him, not with our own capacity, but with the fullness of grace which God bestowed on her.

We understand from this the role of the icon in general and the special role of this icon in the Prayer of the Heart, since it helps us powerfully to enter into the mystery of the Prayer of the Heart and to practice it, whilst greatly reducing the distractions. This icon always comes with a special grace to introduce us into the state of prayer. Whoever experiences praying in front of an icon will thank God for this amazing gift which takes our weakness into consideration.